European Council of Internatior

THE ENGLISH
INTERNATIONAL SCHOOL
Na Okruhu 1, 142 00 Pha 4-Písnice
Tel.: (420 2) 61 91 23 68, 61 91 23 71
Fax: (420 2) 61 91 00 74

Effective Libraries in International Schools

Revised Edition 1999

Carolyn Markuson

Published 1999 by John Catt Educational Ltd,
Great Glemham, Saxmundham, Suffolk IP17 2DH.
Tel: +44 01728 663666   Fax: +44 01728 663415.
E–mail: office@johncatt.co.uk   Internet: http://www.johncatt.co.uk

© 1999 John Catt Educational Ltd.

All rights reserved. No part of this publication may be reproduced, stored in a retrieval system, transmitted in any form or by any means, electronic, mechanical, photocopying, recording, or otherwise, without the prior permission of the publishers.

Opinions expressed in this publication are those of the contributors, and are not necessarily those of the publishers or the sponsors. We cannot accept responsibility for any errors or omissions.

The Sex Discrimination Act 1975. The publishers have taken all reasonable steps to avoid a contravention of Section 38 of the Sex Discrimination Act 1975. However, it should be noted that (save where there is an express provision to the contrary) where words have been used which denote the masculine gender only, they shall, pursuant and subject to the said Act, for the purpose of this publication, be deemed to include the feminine gender and *vice versa*.

A CIP catalogue record for this book is available from the British Library.

ISBN: 0 901577 32 4

Designed and typeset by John Catt Educational Limited,
Great Glemham, Saxmundham, Suffolk IP17 2DH.

Printed and bound in Great Britain by Bell and Bain Ltd, Glasgow, Scotland.

Contents

Foreword, *Kevin Bartlett* 5

Introduction, *Carolyn Markuson* 7

Preface, *Ross J Todd* 9

Chapter 1
Philosophy and Goals 13

Chapter 2
Models of School Library Programmes 16

Chapter 3
Management Manual 33

Chapter 4
Selection, Acquisition and Access Policy 41

Chapter 5
Information Literacy in Action, *Carol Gordon* 43

Chapter 6
Facilities Guidelines 48

Chapter 7
Staff and Evaluation Guidelines 54

Chapter 8
Programme Assessment Considerations 58

Chapter 9
Public Relations, Display and Publicity 61

Appendices . . . . .see over

Postscript 155

Appendices

Appendix A
Action Plan Recommendations   69

Appendix B
Standards and Guidelines   76

Appendix C
Information Literacy Research Models   82

Appendix D
Collection Development & Management   92

Appendix E
Multiculturalism and Multilingualism, *Richard Barter*   98

Appendix F
Staff, Programme and Services Assessment Schemes   107

Appendix G
Library Programme, *John Royce*   112

Appendix H
Selection, Aquistion and Access   124

Appendix I
Adjacencies   133

Appendix J
Library Professionals   136

Appendix K
Library Automation   143

Appendix L
Learning and Information - The Future   150

Appendix M
A Basic Bibliography: Getting Started   153

Foreword: Effective International Schools Series

ECIS is a not for-profit organisation dedicated to the advancement of internationalism through education by the provision of services to its members.

ECIS member schools are spread around the globe and are immensely varied in nature. Yet any of them, new or established, large or small, day or boarding, co-educational or single sex, monocultural or multicultural, can aspire to developing internationally-minded students. The sole proviso as expressed in the ECIS Statement of Philosophy, is that they are committed to the promotion of an international outlook amongst all members of their communities.

ECIS sees its role as providing services, which actively assist schools in working towards this ideal, through practical support. The Effective International Schools series is one way of doing this.

For the purposes of this series, ECIS will restrict itself to those areas of a school's operation with regard to which the Council is in a position to offer sound practical support in the form of documents which offer reliable guidelines and proven examples of good practice. There is much to be gained from sharing the experiences of member schools and little to be gained from reinventing the wheel. Much has been learned since the Council was founded and time, energy and money are too precious to waste. The experience of other schools may offer a real head start.

Each publication will, therefore, have the following elements in common:

* They are driven by a common set of beliefs and values about student learning with an international outlook.

* They are structured so as to illustrate a logical progression from profile to policy to practice.

* They are based on successful experience in international schools, but offer suggestions generic enough to apply in a variety of contexts.

ECIS trusts this series will prove useful to members and welcomes any suggestions for improvements to each publication or for additions to the series.

Kevin Bartlett is Director of Windhoek International School, Namibia

Introduction

Access to information is now global and the impact on libraries has been profound. Curriculum models are changing the instructional models within schools library and information programmes, procedures, and policies are now required to accommodate these new directions if they are to prepare students to be efficient, effective and independent users of the information world.

The revised edition of *Effective Libraries* encompasses all levels of school library services, major developments in information technology and widens the scope to cover all types of international schools.

This revised edition would not have been possible without the writing assistance and valuable collegial support of international school librarians Richard Barter (Lebanon), Coralie Clark (Hungary), Carol Gordon (Germany), and John Royce (Germany), who made substantial contributions to this document. Other librarians who offered advice and counsel included: the late Henry Parker (Japan), Aliki Ammerman (Turkey), Vivienne Warner (Netherlands), Michele Velthuizen (Netherlands), and Linda Marti (Czech Republic).

Special thanks go to Ross Todd of the University of Technology, Sydney, Australia for the informative and 'confidence in the future' preface and to Jennifer Henley, ECIS Guardian Angel, who kept us focused, on track, and willing to explore and expand our horizons!

This edition is dedicated to the memory of Dr W Gray Mattern, whose vision was instrumental in the creation of the original publication.

Carolyn Markuson

Preface

It is my belief, albeit simplistic and idealistic, that schooling is all about providing the best learning opportunities for young people to make the most of their lives as self-directed, self-determining and creative individuals. As schooling meets the third millennium, in an increasingly globalised world of shifting ideologies, cultures, technologies, powers and economies, the challenge of knowing what the best learning opportunities are, and delivering them, is indeed a complex one. And the challenge for international schools, often located within and functioning across diverse cultural, ideological and linguistic boundaries, is no less daunting. Preparing our students today for tomorrow's unknown world, being able to predict an uncertain future, and moving into it with confidence, takes courage and conviction. Indeed, the best way to predict the future is to work towards creating it, and creating it begins today, not tomorrow. This means that although we respect and are informed by our past, we also have the courage and determination to think and act divergently.

Imaginative, informed and transformational leadership is the heartbeat of the future school, and an important key to creating a preferred future. Transformational leadership, identified by Caldwell and Spinks (1995) as the essential leadership in times of rapid change, is transforming and responsive rather than transacting and reactive. It is leadership that is visionary, strategic and collaborative. And it is the kind of school leadership required to confront the unknowns and uncertainties with energy and determination, and to create a preferred future where the best possible learning opportunities are provided for students.

Of the future, however, some things are certain. The world of the learner will increasingly be information rich and information driven, and not just technology rich, rather, technology driven. It will be an ambiguous information world, where the boundaries between rumour, gossip, and that information which is quality and of value, will be blurred, and presented in a technological context where everything looks authentic. And if the current educational literature is an indicator of the future, then the world of the learner will also focus on maximizing opportunities for flexible learning, co-operative learning, collaborative learning, situated learning, contextualised learning, customized learning and transformative learning. While the content of learning will continue to be considered important increasing attention will be given to considering how students learn. In essence, this will focus on valuing the development of metacognitive processes that enable students to effectively, independently and confidently interact with their information-rich and technology-driven world, and to make use of it not just as part of their school-based learning, but as part of their daily lives as well.

Candy, Crebert & O'Leary (1994) characterize independent learners in the following way: they accept responsibility for directing their own futures; they have confidence in their ability to continue learning throughout their lives; they adopt deep rather than surface approaches to learning; they have learned to seek out, analyze, and make meaning out of information; they have developed higher order metacognitive abilities; they are able to transfer the strategies and learning skills into personal and social environments; and they are able to determine what it is they need to know in order to perform particular tasks or to draw meaningful conclusions.

Information is the heartbeat of meaningful learning in schools. In recent years, much attention has been given to the proliferation of information, particularly the provision of electronic information, the rapid growth of the Internet, and the transition from paper to digitized information. For schools, it is acknowledged that the large-scale growth of electronic information sources such as specialized interactive multimedia CD-ROM, the Internet and full-text journal sources will play an increasingly important role in information provision. Yet it is very clear to me that the availability and quantity of this information does not imply learning. Access to vast amounts of information and its associated technology should not be the hallmark of the future school. Rather, a learning environment that empowers students to connect with, engage with and utilize this information in meaningful and purposeful ways should characterize the future school.

The components essential to linking information and learning, and enabling the development of independent, life-long learners, are the intellectual skills and processes required to interact with information in meaningful ways. These involve skills of making decisions about information requirements and judgments about the quality and credibility of information, as well as skills of analysis, synthesis and evaluation of information, and being able to construct new meaning and understanding in the light of new information, experiences and opportunities. It is this interaction that both enables and empowers meaningful learning.

The provision of this learning environment cannot be left to chance. The development of independent learners occurs in a social context where school leaders, teachers, class members, teacher-librarians, and parents provide guidance, feedback and encouragement. It is in an interactive and collaborative context that learners develop initiative and responsibility for the learning process. Fundamental to this learning process is the development of a school-wide information service where learners have opportunities to access multiple sources and forms of information and the appropriate technologies to do so, where and whenever information is needed. It also requires educators who have the professional competencies in information provision and learning; who are able to effectively manage these resources for access; who are able to link information and learning through the development of learners' information handling skills; and who can establish and manage an effective resource and technology infrastructure to support this learning.

In essence, strong library and information services are essential to a learning program that values the cognitive, cultural, social, affective, technological and spiritual development of individuals. The development of information services and their dynamic role in learning requires the highest quality co-operative and responsive support at all levels to ensure that quality buildings, functional facilities, resources and technology, together with a library staff encompassing a range of professional, technical and clerical skills are provided for effective delivery of information services. It will also ensure that purpose and intended outcomes of information provision and services in each school are appropriate to and chosen within the nature, ethos and context of the whole school community.

As part of the school's library and information service, the focal point of the role of the school librarian is the development of students' information and critical literacies, a role not often fully understood and endorsed or capitalized on by the school community. It is a role where the school librarians bring together their knowledge and experience of teaching and learning, their understanding of information and information processes, their abilities to organize effectively and manage information resources and services throughout the school, to provide the highest quality learning opportunities and to enable students to learn best.

This role implies an active engagement in the development of curriculum across all learning areas to ensure the integration of information skills, and a carefully planned library program that is implemented collectively and collaboratively. At the Centre of this library program is the provision of learning opportunities for students to develop information processing, independent research, problem-solving, critical thinking and evaluative skills while using multiple sources and formats of information, including the effective use of information technology.

Against this backdrop, Effective Libraries in International Schools is an open door to the dynamic future of international schools. Its fundamental premise is that the door to the future in these schools is creating an information and learning environment that will enable students, wherever they are, to be part of their rapidly changing world with confidence and certainty. Building on this premise, it provides a thoughtful, pedagogically sound basis for the effective provision of information resources and services in schools, a clear basis for their effective management, and a strong framework for designing learning programs that provide the best learning opportunities for students in a globalized, multicultural and uncertain world.

Ross J Todd, Dept. of Information Studies
University of Technology, Sydney, Australia

Chapter 1

Philosophy and Goals

Every good school library programme must be based on a philosophical statement of beliefs about what the library and its services should be and their place in the institutional scheme. In most schools, such a statement is tacit or assumed, but it is the recommendation here that, on the contrary, each school should develop its own written formulation, at the highest level (though obviously with the participation of all those concerned). The statement then becomes an article of institutional policy, a continuing point of reference to guide the school's Board, administration and professional staff as decisions are taken over the years in respect of such specific matters as facilities, funding, programmes, staffing, *etc.*

Here is a sample statement for a School Library Philosophy, followed by a sample statement of goals for the school library. While these are obviously ideal formulations, they may be modified to suit the particular circumstances of individual institutions.

Statement

The library philosophy of the International School 'X' is derived from the overall philosophy of the school. The broad statements of beliefs the school subscribes to shape the programme and services of the school library.

The school library is an educational and cultural environment where individuals are exposed to ideas through the use of print and non-print resources in many media formats. The school library fosters the development of life-long learning abilities and a love of reading in its students. It also provides teachers with instructional materials and professional resources.

The programme and services evolve directly from the school's curriculum requirements. The library offers an array of resources to implement, support and enhance those requirements, as well as to provide independent leisure reading and its own programme for teaching literary appreciation and information literacy skills.

A trained, qualified professional has four key roles:

> As a **teacher**, the librarian teaches the information curriculum as an integral part of every day classroom instruction. This information curriculum encompasses both an 'information' skills content area – normally thought of as fact-finding and analysis – and a literature-based experience that enriches the common literary heritage and love of reading for all students. The balance between these two aspects of the

programme changes as the student progresses through the grades. The library instructional programme relies on the use of various teaching strategies, a knowledge of student learning techniques, the integration of resources-based instruction, the use of a variety of technological tools, and authentic assessment. The purpose of assessment is to assure that learning is taking place.

As a **programme manager**, key librarian responsibilities include collection development, resource management, and in many schools overall management of the school's information systems technology. This role includes the selection and evaluation of materials that facilitate curriculum implementation, fiscal management, staff supervision, and directs the day-to-day library activities. In order to provide stable accountability of resources within the school as well as to minimise unnecessary duplication, librarians with automated systems are often managers of the resources of the entire school. Whether the resources are housed in the library, in a classroom, or circulate, they are centrally inventoried and easily accounted for with an automated system.

As a **consultant** to the professional staff in the school, the librarian works with and advises students, teachers, and other members of the school community on the availability, appropriateness, and application of the resources to their varied disciplines, levels, and interests.

As a **literature and information specialist,** the librarian encourages and recommends reading, research techniques, and listening and viewing activities appropriate to individuals, groups of students, and faculty, to meet all the learning requirements of the school. Information comes in many forms, and the librarian must be familiar with all kinds of materials, including non-print varieties.

School library goals

Programme goals outline long-range plans for the library and parallel goals set by the school. They are used in the development of the library budget and as a frame for the more specific annual objectives set by the library.

Programme goals for the library are:

Reading/Literature enjoyment and appreciation

- to provide resources and opportunities for students to develop and expand their literary appreciation and reading competence.
- to provide a wide range of resources for the recreational reading, viewing, and listening of students and teachers.

Information Literacy

- to provide resources and consulting services to teachers and students while supporting and enhancing the school's curriculum;
- to provide instruction in the evaluation, selection, identification and use of appropriate information resources in all formats;
- by planning and working directly with classroom teachers, to actively participate in the instructional process in which students use data and information to create new knowledge;
- to provide resources and consulting services to parents and community groups appropriate to the school setting;
- to identify and implement access to resources and information that will enable teachers to implement new teaching strategies;
- to encourage appropriate instructional applications of technologies and provide guidance in their use;
- to effectively and efficiently manage the library facility, resources, and programme to benefit the entire school community;
- to encourage and provide resources that support and extend the multlingual capabilities of the students.

Chapter 2

Models of School Library Programmes

While recognising the variety inherent in international schools, many if not all of these same differences can be found in all corners of the world. Over the past 20 years, it has been generally agreed that quantitative standards, which measure things rather than services and programme, are inappropriate. Rather, it is the instructional programme – the curricula implementation – the teaching and learning process – which sets the standards for library media programmes of the day. Only through this connection will the value and worth of the library investment pay dividends.

A sequence of progressive development is identified in this document.

- The **Foundation** programme provides an initial base line which can grow as the school moves forward toward a more comprehensive and complex curriculum and instructional programme.
- The **Midrange** programme assumes a considerably greater curricular involvement, requires higher levels of personnel and assignment of resources.
- The **Mature** programme will be attained by those schools with strong beliefs in an educational programme that requires a first-class, centrally-important library and information function along with the resources necessary for the support thereof.

The models are all, however, no more than the term implies: they are not specifically prescriptive, but meant to be a constellation of recommendations to be adapted, once again, to the philosophies and beliefs, programme requirements and resources of particular institutions.

It will be noted, too, that while the original publication of this handbook was focused on the pre-secondary years of schooling (because this was the emphasis of the original project in the mid-1980's), this document was written for a pre-school through secondary school continuum.

A team of experienced international school librarians has developed models for school library media services in international schools. These models should not be seen as constituting or replacing standards developed for exemplary programmes by national organisations, but address the differences which these schools face, provide a continuum for development, and in many ways follow the taxonomy of services developed by David Loertscher (1988 - see Appendix G p118) which has a universal applicability.

Suggestions at the Foundation programme are based on *programme* needs rather than *library* needs. The library as an entity supports and extends the classroom, and at the same time teaches its own curriculum of information literacy skills and literary appreciation. Schools with Foundation programmes must require that service to students takes precedence over all other activities, including the organisation of the library itself, for it is in this way that the instructional needs of students can be met. It must be stated, however, that Foundation programmes in no way contribute what upper level services can and do to the educational programme for students.

Many schools include in their statements of mission or philosophy a statement to the effect that the school's library is at the heart of the curriculum. They frequently include comments on information literacy, required as a 'basic skill' for 21st century humankind. The models thus become to some extent indicators of the seriousness of the statements and the value the school places on the learning programme. In the light of several recent research studies, library/media budgets (resources and professional staffing) were shown to provide the highest correlation (of any indicator) to student achievement. The rich contribution of the library made possible the instructional programme that enabled students to improve achievement. Schools, therefore, need to strive to provide the highest possible models of library service for their students.

Comments

Some general comments, based on observations at the international schools and communications with a considerable number of librarians in similar institutions, may be helpful at the outset.

1 The international school community has a wide range of library staffing patterns, collections and facilities. In addition, where professional staff exists, educational preparation varies widely, non-professional 'librarians' span the gamut from trained teachers to untrained volunteers (library aides).

2 There is generally an increasing awareness that the school library programme should be a dynamic, exciting component in the educational process for all children, at all stages of their schooling.

3 Using non-professional staff to lead the library programme is done at great cost. While some excellent people are in place, the demands of a vibrant, exciting programme require that they seek or be provided with training, or, at the least, regular guidance from a professional. Fundamental skills required of anyone being considered to run a school library programme are:
    - a knowledge of teaching methods and strategies
    - ability to develop and teach a sequential skills and literary appreciation programme

- a basic knowledge of child affective and cognitive development
- a fundamental knowledge of children's and young adult literature as well as information resources in many formats, including electronic
- knowledge of electronic information resources and search techniques and expertise with all types of technologies
- sound organisational, managerial, communication, and interpersonal skills.

Professional librarians lacking these skills will, in most cases, find numerous components of the modern school library programme beyond their reach unless they seek further training and education. This is of enormous benefit in enabling the librarian to be accepted by teachers as an equal partner in the educational process.

4 Part-time programmes are just that. They will never make a significant contribution to the educational process or instructional programmes at the school. Though they may benefit a few individual students their limitations remain.

5 In many of the non-professionally-run programmes, there is an inappropriate focus on the mechanics of organising and managing the library (facility and collection). The instructional aspects of the programme place a distant second, if at all. In an educational setting, it is more important to provide the instructional and literary appreciation programme than to be concerned about the cataloguing or organisation of resources. In such situations, the non-professional staff should spend their time regularly meeting with children and making the facility a welcoming, inviting place children want to visit, rather than trying to do tasks without appropriate training.

Besides, their time is best spent with students using the resources rather than organising books to sit on shelves unused and unread. Selections should be made by professional staff (librarian or teacher) based on the curriculum and a knowledge of children's literature.

6 Whenever possible, resources should be ordered with cataloguing and processing included. While this increases the cost of individual items, it allows what staff there is to work with students and programme rather than spend their time behind a typewriter or computer. In schools where small non-English-language collections are maintained for students, simple organisation by author may be sufficient; in schools where large non-English collections are maintained, additional clerical support must be considered, to allow the librarian to work with the books and children.

7 An exciting, dynamic programme requires more than a library, librarian, facility and collection. It requires a common philosophy that

is embraced and articulated clearly by the Head and the teaching faculty as well as by the librarian. The involvement of teachers with the library programme is as much the responsibility of the school leaders as it is of the librarian.

8   The library should be a bright, colourful, inviting, and welcoming place for students. New construction is not required, but an eye toward making the environment child-centred is. Posters, colourful signs, graphics, *etc* - all make the space more inviting to children. Younger children will enjoy stuffed animals, mobiles, and appropriately sized furniture and shelving.

9   It is more important to have a small collection (2,000) of high-quality resources than a large collection of resources that are badly out-of-date, simply sitting on shelves and giving the illusion that a 'library' exists. School library collections are not archival collections; curriculum changes require frequent shifts in collection development and maintenance. Students should be able to rely on knowing that information gathered from the resources in the library is valid, current, and accurate. They should not have hunt through piles of out-of-date resources to find a current item. In such instances, more is not the equivalent of better!

10 Reference books, though expensive, must be kept current. At the K-Grade 6 level the collection is small, but it is important that it be accurate and appealing. The Grade 7-8 collection begins to add additional types of reference sources, and the cost of the collection is concomitantly more substantial. Reference materials for Grades 9 upward can be very expensive and are increasingly specialised. Once again, it is preferable to have a small collection of key current resources than a large collection of out-of-date books. It is well worth investigating the purchase of encyclopedias on CD-ROM, as they are often considerably less expensive than print versions, can be updated more frequently, and are more appealing to student users. Old resources, including encyclopedias, are also apt to contain now-objectionable racial, sexist, and ethnic stereotypes.

11 The librarian in an international school may have special considerations, which do not necessarily affect school librarians in a national school; these are the more important when the language of the school is not the same as the language of the host country. There may be few resources available in the outside community; local public libraries and schools' library services may have few materials in English, and local bookshops are unlikely to stock a range large enough to support the school's needs.

12 Multicultural international schools must consider also the special needs of their communities; books and other resources may be needed in a variety of mother-tongue languages, and the librarian should be aware of theory and trends with regard to the child's maintenance of the mother-tongue. There should be special regard to the language and culture of the host country, in line with ECIS Accreditation criteria. For additional information on the vital importance of this mission to the effective international school library, please see Appendix E *Multiculturalism and Multilingualism* (Barter, 1997).

A: Foundation Programme and Services

Overview

All programmes of service depend on several components. It is assumed at this level that there is a small collection of quality books available: at least full-time non-professional staff; an area where students can be gathered; access to tables and chairs for seat work; and an attractive space devoted to library use. A procedure manual and selection policy must be established so that staff changes do not necessitate re-inventing the procedures all over again.

Staff

Full-time paraprofessionals assisted by volunteers should be available to keep the library open throughout the school day. Staff should carry out an instructional programme planned by professional faculty or a consultant assigned as mentor to the library.

Programme of services – Elementary grades

Instructional and educational aspects

In the elementary grades, efforts must be concentrated on the instructional and educational aspects of the library programme. Therefore, at this level of school library service, students should be scheduled to use the library with their teachers. This traditional programme calls for at least one 30-minute period each week to exchange resources and to learn/practice recently acquired information skills instruction and implement the library literary appreciation programme. The weekly schedule should allow teachers to augment their assigned times by using the several open periods for extended research, literary appreciation activities, and more frequent reading/research practice opportunities.

Students should be able to borrow and return resources at any time and, in fact, be encouraged to come often and, of course, to read extensively. It is important that teachers remain directly involved, as aides or volunteers cannot adequately carry out the teaching responsibilities and are not sufficiently knowledgeable about students' abilities, disabilities, or interests, not to mention the collection of resources to make productive recommendations. A weekly schedule should be maintained for teachers to sign-up for these open periods.

The instructional programme should consist of reading, viewing and listening experiences, with attention given to appropriate information skills, to create an excitement about learning and instill a love of reading. A formal sequential literature programme should be adopted. It should expose students to high-quality books – the BEST in children's literature, from fairy tales through contemporary classics, including non-fiction, poetry, and biography. Reading logs should be developed by students, along with other activities to encourage prolific reading.

Basic information skills curriculum

Alongside the literature programme should be a basic information skills curriculum, developed in collaboration with the teachers, that can be based on an established programme. Many examples can be found in educational literature and more are appearing on the www. Ideally, information literacy skills should be taught by teachers and library staff together, in relation to the classroom curriculum, at time of need, so that 'library' is not seen as an isolated set of skills.

Where possible, additional periods of activity should be scheduled by teachers on an 'as needed' basis, for more intensive work on specific tools relating to topics under examination in the classroom at the time. To be retained, library information skills must be taught and applied in a relevant, timely manner. Teaching skills in a vacuum has been proven to be unsound pedagogy.

Classroom instructional programme

Where possible, the library programme should mirror the classroom instructional programme. It is important that whoever is in charge of the library regularly makes the rounds of the classrooms, looking at bulletin boards, talking to teachers about forthcoming topics, and in all ways possible aligning the library programme with classroom instruction.

Programme of services – Secondary grades

Reading programme

To be successful, and to be taken seriously by the students, a reading programme at the secondary level needs support from teachers, usually English teachers. Teachers and the librarian can work together to produce lists of recommended reading for each grade level, and to ensure that students read some books from the lists each year.

Information skills teaching

The paragraphs on information skills teaching in the elementary grades also apply here. The library should be available for teachers to schedule classes for research, at time of need. Students need to be taught the skills of information literacy, and to be given ample opportunities to practice these. It is not enough to teach them only in the elementary grades – they need to be taught at higher levels, and regular opportunities provided within the curriculum for applying research skills throughout the high school years.

Collections

English Language collection

Teaching programme The collection should be developed with the teaching programme in mind. Reference and research skills need to be taught with new (less than five years old) resources. Cataloguing should be purchased professionally done – if not for all books at least for a select group of resources – so that students have access to a prototype card catalogue. Computerising the card catalogue and circulation records has proven to expand access to the collections and provide better record keeping.

In addition to making inventories fast and accurate, automation can also provide a framework for collection development as the use of individual items can be tracked. The function of the card catalogue as an index to the collection is important; it is the concept, not the format, that is essential knowledge. The collection should be arranged on shelves with the user in mind. A myriad of small collections should be avoided. A 2000-book collection, carefully developed to meet curriculum goals, is ordinarily considered the minimum required to provide even the smallest school with a working library.

Picture books arranged by first initial of the author's last name, should be attractively and invitingly shelved or stored in bins for ready access by very young children. Chapter books or first readers may be gathered in special areas.

General fiction collections for older elementary students should not be divided or grouped by genre. Access to the genre should easily accomplished through either a card catalogue or an automated system. Other practices to avoid include over labelling the books, separating multiple copies of the same title, and pulling collections for special projects, which short-circuits students learning how to make informed choices on their own. The temptation to isolate small segments of the collection should be resisted, except for short-term, temporary displays. Spine labels can help guide student selection, but foster students' reading only one type of story. By Grade 4, students should be able to make appropriate selections with little adult intervention from an ever-expanding range of resources.

Non-fiction may be arranged by general subject areas (with good signage). It may be all in one single collection at the elementary level, but also may be divided by various grade level sections. However, better readers need access to challenging resources, and *vice versa*. All collections should contain resources that meet the needs of the entire range of student abilities.

A media collection that supports the library literary and instructional programme should be developed including electronic resources that support the library literary and information literacy instructional programme. Access to resources through the World Wide Web greatly enhances in-house collections, but comes with additional responsibilities and costs, such as hardware requirements, software, Acceptable Use Policies, *etc*.

Donated books should be carefully scrutinised and kept only if they meet selection policy standards. Those failing to do so may be set aside in an unrestricted collection without being incorporated into the general library collection. Shelf space is costly and should not be cluttered by resources that often appeal mostly to adults who remember them with fondness or feel that all books are good books – stereotypes and all! A 'swap-shelf' of ephemeral children's and adult titles encourages the sharing of books without cluttering the library.

Weeding The collection should be regularly 'weeded' to discard worn, unattractive, and out-of-date materials, as these are off-putting to young users and can contain misinformation.

Other language collections

Except for a very few schools, these collections will be relatively small and developed to provide limited reading opportunities for students learning a new language, or for young children familiar with the language. These collections may be maintained separately, organised in ways that are similar to the English-language collection, so children can move between the two collections with ease. Interfiling of non-fiction resources with the English-language collection should be considered, to provide factual information for students in a choice of languages.

One should take care not to equate small with unimportant. Children need to see that their mother tongue exists, and is valued by their new community. It is important that they also see their culture represented in their new setting. Original works in a native tongue, or even dual language books, encourage the family to read together. This provides an opportunity for parents to feel comfortable reading to and with their children. Care must be exercised that quality literature is identified for inclusion in bilingual and multilingual collections. In the absence of a children's press or publishing base in the mother tongue language, translations may be the best alternative.

Additional recreational reading can be selected as budget permits from established lists of high quality works. Many library publishers and US school districts produce such lists and in many countries, the best of the local literature is also published in English.

Facilities

The library facility should be attractive, child-centred, cheerful, arranged for students (not adults), have bulletin boards, posters and frequently changing displays highlighting events and people. The concept of libraries as places that actively invite young children to come in and share in the wealth of resources is extremely important.

Budget

Once a 2000-volume basic collection is on hand, the collection needs to be maintained, and potentially expanded. It is most important that a stable budget be built for the library programme. Resources require constant renewal, and this is best done on a continuous cycle. Sporadic budgets result in large segments of the collection becoming outdated at once. As the collection is developed, curriculum innovations will result in establishing different priorities for purchase, for the library collection is built with the school curriculum as a guide. Therefore, when the school initiates curricular changes, provision should be made for the library, as well, to allow its programme to keep abreast of the changes.

It is probably inappropriate here to cite figures for book purchases in international schools. For example, volume discounts offered to domestic school systems are not available, and shipping, insurance, duties, and order-processing costs could be major considerations. It may be helpful to note than an oft-quoted dictum is that minimum funding for the collection should be equal to the cost of two books per student per year. Current average book prices, and recommended levels of spending, can be found in the standards published by various national library associations. It is better to have an under-sized collection of attractive up-to-date materials than to retain old materials to boost numbers. Because materials become worn-out and dated, it is estimated that school libraries need to replace 10% of their collection each year.

Library technology

As technology in society in general, and the academic world in particular, is growing at a phenomenal rate, we need to be preparing students for a future where computers will be everyday tools in their lives. Therefore, even the most basic school library should prepare to fund CD-ROMs, a library automation programme, and Internet connectivity. Where the school has no professional librarian, outside professional advice should be sought when purchasing and installing a library automation programme, to prevent expensive mistakes. Any library starting from scratch should very seriously consider computerisation from the start, saving the later time-consuming task of converting from a paper card catalogue. A library automation programme, correctly installed and used, can save hours of time on routine tasks, enable the library to offer a more efficient service, and provide better access to the collection for the students.

B: Mid-range Programmes and Services

Overview

This model of services finds the librarian actively engaged in connecting with teachers, in addition to developing further the established programme of literary appreciation and information skills. The collection is enriched with more recreational reading as well as more depth, particularly in subject areas used heavily by the teachers. Space is provided to accommodate individual and small-group use in addition to whole classes. Students are encouraged to use the cheerful, attractive facility to study, read, and conduct research.

At this level of education, the librarian should be an integral part of the teaching team, co-ordinating curriculum support and managing the resources (both library and classroom). The collection should include a wide range of leisure reading, from teenage popular fiction to attractive editions of modern and older classics; there should be also be a goodly range of non-fiction information and reference works varying from lower reading level texts augmented by visuals to full, in-depth reference materials. Reference materials should be available in formats that are deemed appropriate to library and the student. Hard copy, CD-ROM, and on-line formats all come with benefits and drawbacks. Making good choices for an individual situation must be based on user needs, ease of access, reliability, space availability, and even staff (as in the case of hard copy periodical collections, which require large amounts of staff time to access and replace items on demand).

The library/resource area should be a pleasant and attractive area in which to work. Arrangement should be functional and there should be adequate space with appropriate sized furniture to accommodate individuals, small groups, and whole classes as they pursue their reading, research, or collaborative efforts.

Staff

A full-time professional librarian will be employed, and aides and/or volunteers will be used. Providing regular, reliable clerical help frees the professional to spend more time working directly with students and teachers.

Programme of services

Building on the Foundation programme, as previously described, the Midrange programme would work with an expanded collection, including relevant periodicals and newspapers as well as appropriate CD-ROM and on-line services. The librarian and support staff (aides, volunteers, student teachers) should be in regular communication with the classroom and participating on curriculum review or development committees. The library staff should know, preferably in advance, which topics are under study, and have a thorough knowledge of the library resources that support them.

Students should be able to use the library without interruption throughout the school day. To avoid overcrowding, an informal booking system should be used, with flexibility and understanding on both sides. The teachers and librarian working on the planning of student projects together can further promote this. This would ensure the availability of sufficient resources for the class, or allow for the development of several work group areas with enough, up-to-date materials to complete the project work satisfactorily. This collaboration also allows a continuum of research and study skills to be part of every lesson, with the librarian and teacher leading and supporting the students as a team.

It is essential that the librarian keeps abreast of relevant developments in technology and on-line services so that these materials can be considered for purchase in the library. It is the role of the librarian to keep the teaching faculty up-to-date on the application and potential use of the software or resources in their classrooms. This can be accomplished with informal, individual contacts, written notes or publications, or through casual conversations in the staff rooms. This in-depth communication will open opportunities for collaborative collection development between the librarian and the teachers and departments.

Collections

The size of the collection should be in line with the recommendations in national and international standards. Full details and further suggestions are listed in the bibliography in the Appendix.

As a very general guide, the collection will be larger than the Foundation model. The reference collection would be expanded with additional specialised and general encyclopedias. Periodicals provide excellent research support, particularly in the sciences. Current reading periodicals should be purchased in hard copy while research or reference periodicals should be accessed through an index. Indexing is essential and periodicals for which indexing is not available need not be retained. CD-ROM provides long-term storage for vast amounts of full-text documents. While microforms remain the permanent storage format of choice by academic institutions, electronic formats are more appropriate to the school library. Upper-level elementary and secondary students should have access to those titles identified as basic to the school library research process (see 'IB Union List of Periodicals' in Appendix D).

Additional selection tools should be used to develop the collection:

Booklist, American Library Association, Chicago;
School Librarian, School Library Association, London;
School Library Journal, R R Bowker, New Providence, NJ;
Multimedia Schools, Online, Inc, Wilton, CT
and on the Internet companies such as Amazon.com which provide book reviews.

Bibliographies of the best in children's literature, such as *Elementary School Library Catalog*, or *Best Books for Children* should be consulted. Publisher catalogues are inappropriate selection tools. The same is true of vendor catalogues, which simply represent the collection they have in the warehouse for sale. A list of selection tools can be found in Appendix D.

If an Opening Day Collection is needed for a new school or for one requiring substantial rebuilding, a list can be prepared by all of the major book vendors. These lists should be based on a group of specific reviewing tools and notable lists as well as specialised lists developed by the school, *eg* an IB list of authors. These, nonetheless, must be carefully reviewed for duplicate titles, out-of-date items, inappropriately labelled grade designations, and either an over abundance of one topic or insufficient depth in another area. They are never a substitute for a knowledgeable librarian, who knows the curriculum and the teaching strategies of the teachers. They are just a first step in selecting a new collection. As a general rule, non-fiction resources constitute the larger portion of the collection in a middle/secondary school.

As the collection is of substantial size, it is necessary that it be indexed in accordance with standard professional classification system and cataloguing rules. Normally, for collections of the size predominate in international schools, the Dewey Classification (or Abridged Dewey Classification) is more than sufficient to use. This classification scheme allows books to be shelved in 'browsing' order, with similar topics shelved together. This also allows for the development of an index to the collection, often spoken of as a 'card catalogue' or, if electronic, an OPAC (Online Public Access Catalogue). For numerous reasons, a computerised library system, rather than a print card catalogue, should be used to provide the index.

New technologies should begin to be included in the development of the collection. Computers will be available to students in the library, as they become proficient in selecting, identifying, reorganising, and presenting data gleaned from their research and reference efforts.

Facilities

Space for class use and for individual and small-group use should be available, preferably in the form of small conference areas. It must be attractive, child-centred, welcoming, and a place in which students and teachers feel comfortable for both instructional and personal use. Student social areas should be made available outside the library. Workspace for the operation of the library is essential. If the library houses equipment, then space for storage, repair, and set-up needs to be provided.

Budget

The budget should be adequate to allow for the expansion of the collection in both breadth and depth, as well as for the regular renewal of out-of-date or worn-out items. The advent of an ever-expanding number of CD-ROM and other non-book resources should also be reflected in the funding. Maintenance agreements, site licenses for CD-ROM networks, software support agreements, on-line charges, and printer/computer supplies are all new budget items required to support adequate service to students and teachers

Library technology

Increased levels of hardware available to students in the library would support extending the collection to provide in-house depth, through an expanded print and electronic collection. CD-ROM workstations, perhaps a CD-ROM or DVD Tower with high storage hard drives to distribute resources on a computer network would be included, as would a total library automation software package. www and Internet resources would be available to augment the in-house holdings. Again, the collection and equipment would meet and be an integral part of the overall technology plan for the school. Policies and procedures would be in place to support this form of resource acquisition. High speed modems and phone lines would provide efficient access and excellent downloading capabilities.

C: Mature Programmes and Services

Overview

The optimum library programme is situated at the centre of the educational process. It is a proactive programme, involved in curriculum development, team planning and teaching. It provides resources for the classroom, and offers both assistance and direction for curriculum revision and redirection.

Staff

There will be professional, paraprofessional and clerical staff to support the multitude of activities provided by the centre.

Programme

Mature programmes further extend the activities found in Foundation and Midrange programmes. The close co-ordination with the classroom includes:
- curriculum development and team teaching;
- sharing in the responsibility of grading students' papers and projects;
- the design and development of instructional materials used in the class room as well as the library (instructional design);
- and an extensive information-skills programme involving search strategies, resource evaluation, and multimedia-media production skills.

In such programmes, the librarian contributes to the overall planning and structure of the school.

Collection

The size of the collection is again increased to meet in-depth research needs and the demands of a sophisticated and varied curricula. Resources used by the teacher to design instruction will also be included, such as electronic and telecommunication resources. New technologies will be evaluated and used when deemed to further enhance and develop classroom instructional opportunities and support, as well as provide research/reference resources for students and teachers. Again, the currency of the collection remains important.

Core collection of periodicals

Three studies in the US in the 1980s and a recent survey of IB schools in 1995 have been made to determine the basic reference/research journals used by secondary school students. The results are summarised in Appendix D.

Facilities

The space available should include areas for classes, small groups and individuals. In addition, there should be work space for the production of multimedia, video and mechanisms for its distribution to classroom. Work space is also needed for storage and repair of computers, as well as room to organise and store kits and resources developed in-house for classroom instructional use.

Budget

The budget for a Mature programme would include all the items in a Midrange programme, but at increased levels of intensity. A frequently suggested recommendation for the exemplary library/information programme is that 10% of the per-pupil operating cost be assigned to this aspect of the school's schedule of expenses. It has been suggested that schools begin to consider technology upgrades at this level be incorporated into the operating budgets of the school, rather than part of capital expenditures.

Library technology

There would be a total integration of print, nonprint, and electronic information resources carefully selected to meet the needs of students and the instructional strategies of the teachers. This would build on and expand the resources and access to workstations found in earlier programmes. Services could include on-line or off-line www searching, satellite delivery of information and distance learning opportunities. Network access to the collection should be from any computer workstation in the school, as well as from the home.

Changes in video access from analogue to digital will result in new dimensions of video services to schools and homes. The ability to deliver video-on-demand directly to the 'desktop' opens opportunities for worldwide access to information and instructional programs, virtually at an instant's notice. Staff development, meta-field trips all become possible to schools ready to receive them. The library then becomes a virtual information centre, with resources available where and when students or faculty deem it necessary. As technology advances, new applications would become an integral part of the library and information programme.

Chapter 3

Management Manual

Whatever level of services a school is able and prepared to provide, it is extremely useful to have a *Library Management Manual*, a kind of 'bible' always available for ready reference in respect of any matter having to do with any aspect of the library programme. Particularly in international schools, where mobility amongst all sections of the community is endemic, this sort of document can save an enormous amount of time, money, energy, and frayed nerves. New librarians will not have to re-invent the wheel; new Heads will discover immediately the place of the library programme in the life of the school and what to expect of it; new teachers will learn their roles in interaction with the library; and new Board members will know what is in place in this important area of school function and what provisions must be made for its maintenance and improvement.

Like all policy manuals, the *Library Management Manual* must derive and proceed from the school's basic beliefs about its mission and the manner of function. It must reflect governance style, the idiosyncrasies of the particular community, and most particularly its currently available and potential resources of all kinds. It must be carefully crafted to embody the wisdom and knowledge of those immediately concerned, the professional cadre, as well as the experience of comparable institutions (it will not be the first school *Library Management Manual* ever written!) But it should as well reflect the insights of all those on whose functions and responsibilities the library and its programme will impinge. It's no good having the librarian sit down and write the whole document over the next summer break; unless, at the end of the process, it reflects the agreement of the whole community, it will not have the necessary force and authority and usefulness.

The policy manual should be regarded as a working document – unlike the sacred writ, not immutable, but under constant review, subject to modification and up-dating as perceptions and circumstances change, though with proper provision that such changes be made only after thorough consideration and with appropriate authority.

The section that follows provides, in effect, a practical how-to-do-it guide. It indicates all of those elements, which should be included in a good *Library Management Manual*, and suggests in each section, the kind of questions and concerns which should be addressed. Carefully used, it will permit a school to create for itself a document tailored to its own needs. The process itself will be enormously valuable in helping a school to focus on what sort of library programme it should have. The end result will surely be a new understanding of the importance of this aspect of the institutional function, along with some powerful assurance that it will continue to command the attention so vital an aspect of the teaching and learning process deserves.

Library Management Manual Contents

Introduction

The *Library Management Manual* codifies the policies and procedures of the library media centre (LMC) to provide for the orderly functioning of the LMC programme and services. The manual is particularly useful in organising one's thoughts about the role of the centre in the school, and in providing an operational continuum for new staff. It can be used as an orientation tool for new administrators, teachers, or volunteers, by outlining the basic plan of the programme and services offered by the library media centre programme.

Setting

The section on the setting describes the local community, the school, and the curriculum. A copy of the school catalogue and course of study may suffice. A map of the local area, suggestions on shopping, living, transportation, *etc* may be included if deemed appropriate.

Philosophy

All schools will have, or certainly should have, their own statements of basic philosophy (Accredited schools are required to have such statements). The school library media centre philosophy must be in agreement with the school philosophy. (For a simple statement, see Chapter 1 of this guide).

Planning

There are two broad types of planning that are important to the school library media programme. One, strategic planning, informs the school community of teachers and learners why the library does what it does in fairly broad terms, while operational planning leads to programme outcomes. When thought of as behavioural outcomes (what will students be able to do, or be doing?) these outcomes become benchmarks in the development of the programme and provide a framework on which to build progressively more responsive and interactive programmes for teachers and students.

These two plans are interdependent. The operational plan could be considered the yearly plan, assessed on progress from the year before and looking toward the year hence. The strategic plan includes defining and/or redefining a core mission statement (why does the library exist? what is its role?) and assessing programme needs (what does it need to meet its goals and objectives?). The operational plan is most concerned with defining key information needed for decision-making (curriculum, culture, teaching strategies, changed learner needs), with assigning responsibility for personnel (drawing on staff strengths), and with defining the goals and objectives (what the programme stakeholders or constituents want accomplished because of the programme).

Programme planning ultimately translates into fiscal terms. It both justifies the financial load of particular programme areas and activities as well as identifies clearly the fiscal inputs required to meet the demands of the agreed upon core mission. Planning leads to budget development which in turn results in readjustments to plans. Simplistic annual budget adjustments are counterproductive to planning and are tantamount to merely a tedious recycling of the status quo.

Programme development

The programme of services offered by the library media centre grows out of the goals of the school and should be included in the multi-year planning process. Objectives should be drafted yearly, reflecting the curricular activities (or changes) of the school as well as the management aspects of the centre itself (weeding the collection, automating the circulation, developing a computerised card catalogue, *etc.*) The library management tasks of the centre are not ends in and of themselves, but rather the means of delivering better services and instructional programmes. The planning and objectives provide accountability for the programme. (See sample Goals Statement in Chapter 1)

Role of standards

Several standards can be used as measures, *eg*, the self-evaluation forms of recognised accrediting agencies, professional association standards, government guidelines, or other agreed-upon norms (regional, corporate, *etc*). Where one stands in relation to established norms is one form of evaluation. The school library literature of the United States and the United Kingdom is in general agreement on the role of the library. However, a recently reported (1996) study conducted by the International Federation of Library Associations (IFLA) noted that few countries had either official governmental or association guidelines or policy statements governing the development of school libraries. While it is important that the international school look to its host country for information, the curriculum of the individual school will undoubtedly require guidelines or standards from 'home.' For example, if the school supports an IB programme, the IB guidelines would be essential; if an American curriculum, guidelines from the American Association of School Librarians and the Association for Educational Communication and Technology (AASL/AECT) would be appropriate.

The various Internet sites of national library associations may provide information about the most current frameworks for assessing programmes.

Resources (procedures)

This part of the Management Manual answers the question 'How do we do it?' It is very school-specific and codifies the procedures used to achieve each area.

Some of the questions that might need answers include:

Selection How are the resources selected? Who makes the final decisions? How are the teachers and students involved in the process? Are software resources previewed before purchase? Which selection tools are used to identify high-quality new resources? What format is needed? Is more than one format needed? Should this be an on-line product, or should we own it outright? (See Chapter 4, Selection, Acquisition and Access Policy.)

Acquisitions Where are the orders placed? How is the 'on-order' file organised? Who maintains this file? What specifications are established for processing, *etc*? How long is an order open? Are purchase orders cut for a specific amount ('Do not exceed $/£/LIt/FF/DM')? When does one re-order materials that did not arrive? How are out-of-print, out-of-stock, not-yet-published reorders handled?

Purchasing How are orders written? What forms are used, if any? What must accompany the purchase order (a list, collection of 3" x 5" order cards, *etc*)? What accounts are used for books, audio-visual or computer software, periodical, *etc* orders? Are funds for 'books ordered but not received' automatically returned to the appropriate account? Can you encumber funds for future use? How often may you order (as needed, once or twice per school year, *etc*)? How can an order be cancelled? Is there a bid sent to vendors to encourage higher discounts?

Evaluation Is there a preview process for software? (As this may not be possible or overly time consuming, an alternative is finding reviews, posting questions on listservs, calling a colleague, or requesting a 'return' in the event that it is unsatisfactory.) Are areas of the collection evaluated against standard tools? How are gifts evaluated? Is a list of acquisitions kept, arranged by Dewey (or other system) numbers, to see what kinds of balance new orders represent? Are you ordering too many picture books – fiction – social studies – sufficient science – or biographies *etc*? Are comments solicited from the teachers and students regarding the collection? Do you need duplicate copies? If an electronic or on-line

version exists, which is chosen or are different (multiple) formats needed?
Professional/special collections Does the library co-ordinate the purchase of these collections? Where are they housed? How are selections made? Are they organised differently from the general collection?
Organisation How is the collection organised and arranged for students to use? Are 'breakaway collections' (groups of materials that are shelved in a special area) identified in the card catalogue or OPAC (electronic card catalogue), *eg* fairy tales, fantasy, science fiction, myths, mysteries? How are these books or those for 'just new' or non-readers arranged?
Classification and cataloguing What classification system is used? What subject-heading system is used? Are all materials classified and catalogued alike (vertical file, professional collection)? What specifications have been given to vendors who provide materials already processed? What rules are adjusted for this particular library? What about biographies, short-story collections? Are joint authors used – filed? Illustrators – producers (software)?

Are MARC records used? If automated, is there a procedure manual for adding new entries and removing old ones? Does the circulation automation include an OPAC (on-line public-access catalogue)? What notations are made in the books/media? What notations are used on the shelf-list card, if any? What is typed on the card and pocket? If automated, what changes are made in the processing – book cards and shelf list are no longer needed?. Is the ISBN number recorded, and where? Are special colour cards used and, if so, where, when and why? Are paperbacks fully processed?
Filing What rules are followed – modified – ignored? (If a book of filing rules is used, such as the ALA Rules for Filing Catalogue Cards, 2nd ed., abridged, 1968, a referral suffices).
Maintenance and repair (equipment) Where are repairs made? How are they arranged? Are records kept on each piece of equipment? When is a piece of equipment considered disposable? Are supply and lamp inventories maintained? Is equipment inventoried – engraved – labelled? Where is it stored? How often are inventories done? Who does them? How do you report lost or stolen equipment? How is it replaced? What does the inventory card (if there is one) include (serial number, model number, price, source, date of purchase, location, *etc.*)? For computers additional information should be kept, *eg* memory, disk capacity, where the backups are, how often software and files are backed up (never often enough!), peripherals *etc.*
Gifts How are donated materials handled? Are the materials catalogued? How are those that do not meet selection criteria handled? How are inappropriate or otherwise unwanted resources treated?
Weeding How is the currency of the collection maintained? Is there a systematic process that continually removes out-of-date or seldom-used resources? How are teachers involved?

Arrangement How are resources arranged on the shelves? (This is often noted on a 'library map' and posted for student use).
Replacement How are replacements made, if at all? Is there a schedule for equipment and resource replacement?

Organisation for use

This section of the *Library Management Manual* details the rules and regulations of the library media centre. It also includes the myriad of records the library is expected to keep on
- activities and users
- procedures for circulating resources
- how to arrange some of the services – teacher involvement in selection of resources – schedule instructional skills classes *etc.*
- and what statistics are kept and how they are used, *eg,* the number of classes taught, reference questions asked, types of skills taught, monthly report forms, yearly reports, *etc.*

As the programme evolves, so must the organisational structures and procedures that support that programme.

Instructional programme

The instructional skills sequence details the literature and information skills programme for students. Services specifically intended for teachers and their classes must be established, along with simple procedures enabling teachers to know how to take advantage of the services (See Chapter 5, Information Literacy in Action).

The instructional programme for teachers and administrators includes a comprehensive plan for in-service opportunities.

Are records kept of student achievement? Are assignments collected? Pathfinders developed? Lesson or unit plans written to accompany bibliographies or instructional periods?

Facilities

An annotated floor plan of the library helps students and staff locate resources quickly and efficiently. Is signage clear? A cheerful atmosphere? Are bulletin boards changed frequently? (See Chapter 6, Facilities Guidelines.)

Staff

The responsibilities of the library staff are established in job descriptions. Responsibilities of volunteers and student assistants should be identified, either in a job description, or in a list of activities normally assigned to such staff. Through these documents, staff becomes aware of other expectations for the library programme.

If an evaluation plan is in effect, staff should be aware of the plan and its implementation. (See Chapter 7, Staff and Evaluation Guidelines.)

Communications and public relations

One of the most important tasks of the library staff is to keep the school community aware of the opportunities offered by the library programme of services. This can be done through informal means, such as memos, or brief faculty meeting presentations. However, it is a continuous process, as faculty, parents, and students come and go. Therefore, it is prudent to establish some formal, regular mechanisms for regularly apprising the school and parent community of the activities, opportunities, and resources of the library media centre.

Budget planning

The budget is a statement of the programme in financial terms and is established by a continuous process of evaluation. Changes in curriculum, the student body, the library media centre multi-year programme plan, and the cost of repair/replacement of resources and equipment dictate the development of a fiscally prudent budget plan. The programme objectives determine the timeline for purchases during a given financial year. Changes in budgets must be accompanied by justifications in terms of programme or instructional outcomes.

Revision

A system for regular review and modification of the *Library Management Manual* should be described. It must specify clearly who has responsibility and authority for what aspects of the review and modification process, as well as any regular schedule and procedures to be followed.

Appendices

Relevant contacts names, addresses, and phone numbers of essential local services or community contacts, book or other resource suppliers, equipment sales and service, colleagues in the region, *etc.*
Professional reference shelf course catalogue, book and software selection tools, library-skills activity books, bibliographies, supply catalogues, vendor and publisher catalogues, cataloguing and classification resources, management manual, and periodical listings are some of the resources required by the library media specialist.
Policy statements including selection policy, AUPs, controversial issue handling (if not a part of the selection policy), copyright, etc. A governing body formally approves these.
Procedure statements, the how-to-do-it section that helps provide

information on the processes that need to be followed in the day-to-day operation of the library media centre. These change as the programme matures, so frequent review and revision is necessary. These are, therefore, the means by which the policies are carried out.

Chapter 4

Selection, Acquisition, and Access Policy

All schools should have an approved selection, acquisition, and access policy. This policy governs how materials are acquired or accessed electronically, and defines the criteria upon which purchase or access decisions are based. Such a policy serves many additional purposes, which include:
- keep the school community fully informed on specific practices of the school
- guide the development of collections that will support and enrich the curriculum
- assign responsibility for the selection of resources and the development of the collections
- provide a means of handling challenges of censorship and pressure groups
- co-ordinate the development of the information resources available and accessible for the students
- establish the basis for gift handling procedures.

To implement the development of a policy statement, the librarian will
- explore with the Head (and other appropriate members of the administrative staff if any) the need for a policy and the means to establish one
- serve on a committee appointed by the Head to draft a statement
- acquire and distribute to the committee the resources and background information needed to develop the policy statement
- participate in the drafting and revision of a policy statement.

The contents of the policy should
- include a statement of the delegation of responsibility for the selection of books and materials
- establish a procedure for responding to criticisms or requests for review of particular materials
- apply to all resources, regardless of format, *eg* film, video, book, periodical, microform, artefacts and objects, computer software, *etc*
- state the purpose of the collection, *eg*, foster excellence in all disciplines associated with the school's educational philosophy, guide students to master skills, to acquire knowledge, and to think critically, creatively, and independently, meet individual and class needs, meet varied levels

of ability, offer differing points of view, and provide relevant, efficient and cost effective access to either acquisitions or planned access via electronic means
- cite the criteria used in selecting resources, *eg* educational significance, contribution to curriculum, favourable reviews, reputation of author, valid content, timelines, contribution to representative viewpoints on issues, appropriateness to the grade-level, pertinence to emotional and social development of the students, suitability for differing learning and teaching styles, artistic or literary quality, and others appropriate to a particular school (*eg* mother-tongue collections), *etc*
- direct the staff to prepare procedures to be followed in selecting and developing a collection to meet the instructional and recreational needs of the student and teaching body. This includes all steps from initial screening to final selection; the reviewing tools (books and periodicals) used; consultations with teachers, students, and possibly the parent community; where resources are purchased; how gift materials are to be handled; cataloguing instructions if any; and replacement/weeding criteria and process.

This policy should be regularly reviewed and revised as necessary. The librarian should ensure that the administration and representative teachers are familiar with the contents, and are interpreting the policy in the same way. This will help to ensure a rational rather than an emotionally charged approach to resolve a complaint, if and when a resource or access to externally obtained material (*eg*, on the Internet) is challenged.

Acceptable Use Policy

Schools offering access to the Internet should establish a Board policy that defines the educational applications of the Internet and www for their students. This policy statement may include different means of access for different age levels of students. For example, primary students would access the www through previously identified sites, an intranet, or locally developed database of web resources; middle and upper level students would have increasingly wider access to the open www, and perhaps individual email accounts.

As an integral part of this policy, students and faculty would sign an Acceptable Use Policy (AUP). The purpose of this AUP policy is to specify the potential educational role of the Internet, particularly in the development of information literacy skills, outline appropriate use of this extensive resource, and provide guidelines for appropriate etiquette while working in a 'virtual environment.' The policy would include mention of the need to educate young people in the responsible use of electronic information sources. It should encourage students to be self-monitoring, in that they should agree not to misuse the service provided by the school to deliberately accessing non-educational sites. Examples of AUP policies are included in Appendix H.

Chapter 5

Information Literacy in Action

Carol Gordon

Library instruction aims at helping learners understand the process of seeking information that leads to knowledge in an increasingly complex and rapidly changing information-rich environment. Planning and building an effective library instruction programme in an international school is facilitated by a blueprint with specifications that can be customised to the needs and resources available at the school site. The effectiveness of such a blueprint will be enhanced if it fits into the educational landscape of 'current best practice' in the field of education at-large.

What follows then is not a plan for a programme but tools for designing information literacy instruction for Foundation, Mid-Range and Mature level programmes. A survey of current trends in classroom and library teaching and learning establishes the optimum environment for such a programme. Examples of standards (learning outcomes) for information skills are presented as building blocks for information skills curriculum documents that are 'transparent,' *ie* skills are embedded in subject area curricula and taught through the subjects. In addition, strategies for implementing the research process and examples of assessment instruments illustrate how guidelines set by current trends channel teaching strategies.

The educational landscape – what's the best practice? The critical skills initiative provided an excellent framework for the assessment of library instruction (Mancall, Aaron, & Walker, 1986) as the integrated, or process approach to teaching library schools became the prominent strategy for librarians (Kuhlthau, 1988). Inquiry was defined as, 'a complex process that includes formulating a problem or question, searching through and/or collecting information to address the problem or question, making sense of that information, and developing an understanding of, point of view about, or answer to the question' (Sheingold, 1987, p 2). Inquiry learning, as it inevitably spilled out of the classroom, impacted the librarian who, 'as teacher must not only be concerned with demonstrating expertise as an instructor, but must resist the traditional classroom routines which prevent free inquiry from taking place' (Callison, 1986)

Libraries were seen as appropriate places for integrating skills and resources across the curriculum and for affording students opportunities to become proficient in inquiry (Kuhlthau, 1987). The constructivist view of learning, whereby the learner constructs meaning rather than passively absorbing facts, fuelled these initiatives to promote thinking and the use of resources to build on prior learning (Ausabel, 1963). Project work emerged as a dominant paradigm for library programmes as inter-disciplinary units became the battle cry in middle schools (Jacobs, H. H., 1989).

Two seminal questions dominate current literature and practice... 'What should students know and be able to do?' The other involves rethinking assessment practices and addressed the question, 'What do students know and what are they able to do?' (Soodak & Martin-Kniep, 1994, p.184). Performance assessment, also known as authentic assessment, emerged as a constructivist tool for designing authentic tasks that were meaningful. These grew from curriculum objectives, and were often interdisciplinary, whereby learners used the tools of the expert in problem solving and decision making learning situations with opportunities for display, presentation and sharing of outcomes.

Recent educational developments in assessment have questioned the traditional assessment techniques and established criteria and guidelines for alternatives (Wiggins, 1992). Traditional pencil and paper tests 'are based on views of learning and knowing that are not best suited to the development needs of adolescents' while methods such as concept mapping 'provide a rich view of student knowledge' (Dana & Tippins, 1993, p.3). Diagnostics (tests that are performance based) are indistinguishable from the authentic tasks themselves and provide continuous feedback to both students and teachers. The projects and active learning initiatives of the previous decade are upgraded to authentic tasks and assessments: they inform the learner, who is assessed rather than graded, for strengths and weaknesses, and the teacher, who adjusts instructional strategies based on student performance.

The emphasis on authentic assessment has profound implications for library programmes as the concept of assessment moves away from the exclusive use of paper and pencil testing and grading and towards viewing assessment as collecting evidence for feedback to learners and teachers through rubrics, portfolios and other formative, or diagnostic instruments, *ie*, tests that are performance based. These initiatives are good news for librarians as they collaborate with teachers who are looking outside their classrooms to design learning situations and assessments that are conducive to active and authentic learning.

Information literacy and information skills

Information literacy has emerged as an overriding issue in library instruction (Irving, 1985). It is described as a need-driven goal which integrates knowledge of tools and resources with skills and exists independently, but relating to, literacy and computer literacy (Brevik, 1985). Information literacy raises levels of awareness of the knowledge explosion and how information is organised.

An information literate student is an avid reader; a critical and creative thinker; an interested learner; an organised investigator; an effective communicator; a responsible information user; a skilled user of technology tools (Loertscher, 1996).

Information skills, encompassing literacy, learning to learn, library literacy, information literacy, and computer literacy is a broad term incorporating a range of subordinate or prerequisite skills: those associated with reading, writing, searching, retrieving, organising, processing, thinking, analysing, and presenting. They include hundreds of skills that fall into categories such as researching, studying, computing and retrieving information that are integral to thinking skills ranging from recognition, recall and memorising to analysing, synthesising and evaluating. Information skills are synergistic and context-dependent: one skill depends on another, and they are all grounded in the content of academic disciplines. Most importantly, the skills evolve from content area objectives that are rooted in the major concepts of the subject disciplines themselves. Figure 1 illustrates how content area objectives power a programme that is need-driven and classroom centred. While information skills drive the library instruction programme, they are not its starting point. They serve instead as touchstones for information literacy, connecting what is happening in the classroom with what can happen in the library/computer lab.

Information skills range from the mechanics of using an index or word processing programme to higher level thinking skills. These lists are amorphous as well, responding to rapid changes in technology and information delivery systems. An effective information literacy programme does not take root in a list of skills dictated by a scope and sequence that is pre-determined and out of the context of the school's fertile curricular environment.

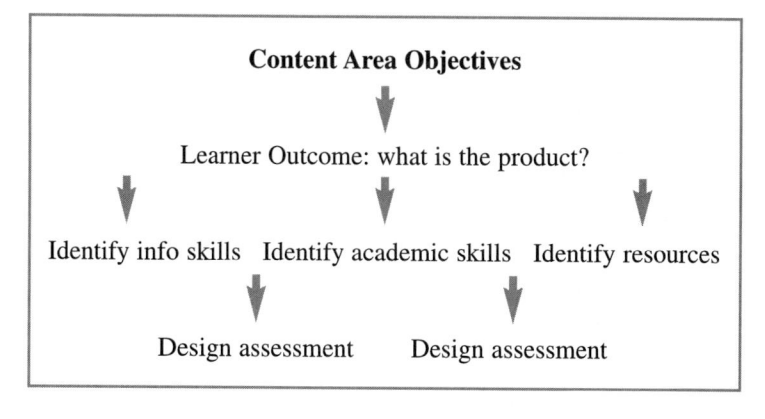

Content Area Objectives
↓
Learner Outcome: what is the product?
↓ ↓ ↓
Identify info skills   Identify academic skills   Identify resources
↓ ↓
Design assessment   Design assessment

Figure 1: A model for the classroom-library connection

Nor can an effective programme grow from skills lists that ignore the affective and metacognitive aspects of learning. Any standards, or goals, that attempt to describe what we would like learners to know and be able to do must start with the learner. Instruction and curriculum converge as teachers and librarians decide what the learning priorities are. Study and information skills cannot be represented by one curriculum 'area'; they are the substance of all academic work and a great deal of non-academic work in schools. (Irving, 1985, p14).

The process of building strong connections between academic work and information skills is essentially the same whether students are key word searching in an electronic index or using a print index, *eg* Readers' Guide. The point is that learners are doing meaningful work using information skills while crossing curricular boundaries. Assignments then are student-centred, interdisciplinary, authentic tasks that are project-based and authentically assessed. Skills are selected and presented in a context that enables learners to perform authentic tasks.

Generic information skills lists are best used when they are customised, through selecting, categorising and labelling target skills, to meet academic needs and accommodate grade levels, using the facilities and resources available. Figure 2 presents five categories of information skills from an integrated library/information technology programme for middle schoolers that operates in a Mature library programme.

Information Skills

↓

Selecting, Labelling and Categorising

↓

| Personal Management | Information Retrieval | Study Skills and Learning to Learn | Research Skills and Thinking Skills | Computer Skills |

↓

Information Literacy (Library) Currculum Documents

↑

Academic (content area) Subjects

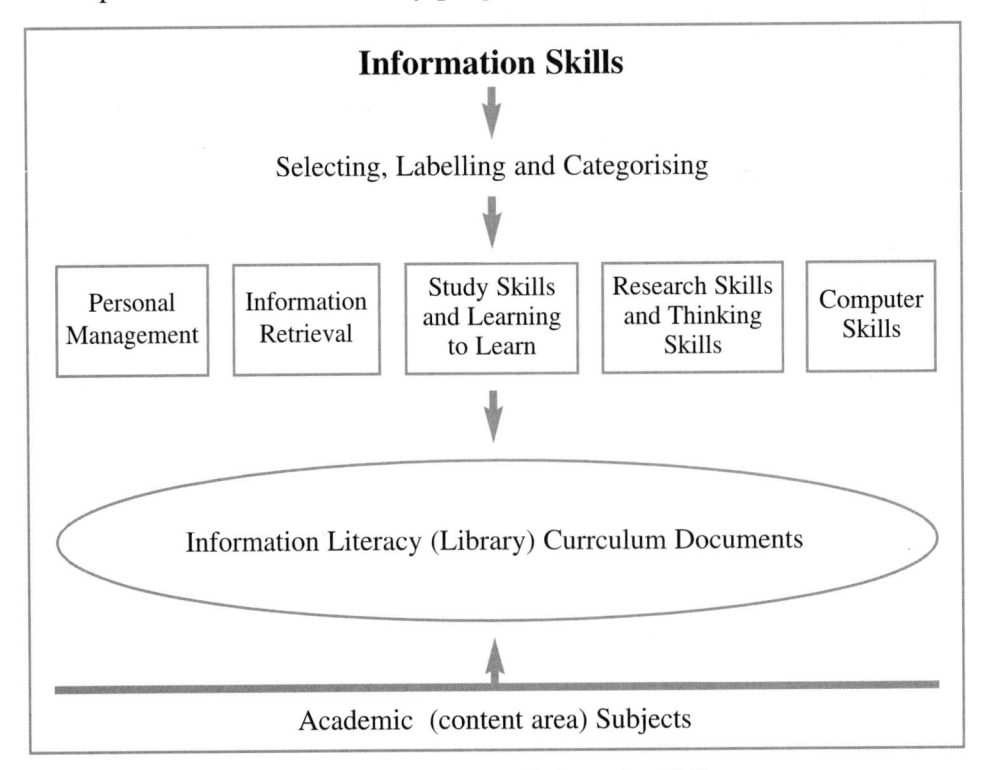

Figure 2: Categories of Information Skills

These categories as, well as the skills that are selected to appear in an information literacy curriculum document, structure the library instruction programme and present opportunities for interaction between the classroom and the library. Resources and facilities may limit the scope of categories of information skills that can be included in project work (*ie*, computer skills are tool-based). However, thinking skills that provide depth and are related to the subject area, or academic context, in which information skills are embedded, are not tool-based and should not be excluded.

All library programmes can be highly integrated and project-based. In fact, such a programme on the Foundation level is easily adapted to include technology when the facilities and resources of the electronic medium become available. Librarians can ensure that all learners have opportunities to practice seminal information skills.

Plagiarism

Designing developmentally appropriate tasks that include higher level thinking skills is apparent in the shift from reporting to researching, or investigating any question or problem, as learners move from elementary to secondary grades. Learners who are stuck in the reporting mode are vulnerable to plagiarism as the result of poorly designed assignments that require nothing more than the regurgitation of information.

Students plagiarise because they are taught to do research under a faulty instructional model (Davis, 1994). This faulty model is a linear one, *ie*, choosing a topic, narrowing that topic, locating information, taking notes, organising notes, writing the paper (Kuhlthau, 1984) rather than viewing these stages as reflexive. Full-text databases that generate printouts of text are perceived by the teacher to encourage plagiarism: students prefer to highlight text rather than take notes. It may be those underdeveloped critical thinking skills and poorly designed assignments are responsible, in some part, for the prevalence of plagiarism.

Carol Gordon, Frankfurt International School, Germany
1998

Chapter 6

Facilities Guidelines

The design of library media centre facilities has a major impact on how well they serve the school: facilities must be accessible, well organised, adequate in size, and attractive. Most basic considerations are the same in planning for either a new or remodelled facility. At the very first instance of conceptualising the need for a library facility, planning is essential. The educational philosophy of the school, together with the philosophy and role of the library media services, must be examined. Current and future curriculum plans and their integration with the library media centre programme and resources must be considered.

In creating a workable facility, the planning stage is crucial and should involve a broad range of staff in addition to the library staff. Changes resulting from the impact of technology on information must be considered. Drawing a floor plan, placing the collection (on paper), testing the 'flow of traffic' as students move through the centre, and looking at adjacencies (what areas need to be next to or in close proximity with one another) are essential components of the planning and, ultimately, the evaluation processes.

Scenarios should be developed to acquaint the architect with what daily life in the centre is like, remembering that today's library media centres bear little or no resemblance to those the architects encountered when in school. Care should be taken to assure that the facility is designed to promote the programme and to deliver the services demanded by the educational programme as it evolves in the future. It is not, nor should it be, a static entity but a vital, vibrant component reflecting the instructional beliefs of the school community.

General Considerations

Location

Preferably near the centre of the school, for easy access. The centre should have an outside entrance for possible use outside of school hours. Access is easiest if at ground level for deliveries. If a multi-level facility is planned, provision for mechanically moving books and materials between levels must be provided in addition to the visual sight lines required for supervision.

Accessibility

Every student should have access to the library facility. This may involve ramps and elevators. This is not only for general use, but also for emergency emptying in case of fire, *etc.* Handicapped faculty and staff need to be able to use the facility with ease.

Environment

The decor must be inviting to students and teachers, with visual appeal. Signage needs to be clear and prominent. Furnishings must be chosen to balance aesthetic appeal with durability and usefulness over a long period of time. With the advent of technology, additional ergonomic considerations need to be borne in mind.

Orientation

If one has any say in the matter, the orientation of the library is more than a personal choice. Southern exposures in the northern hemisphere and *vice versa* for southern hemisphere schools invite abundant heat and sunlight into the room. Skylights too often reflect heat and light onto work areas with similar results. East and west windows bring morning and afternoon sun and, where present, influence the placement of computers, TV monitors, reading and work areas.

With all this in mind however, it is important to remember that libraries are people places and need to be designed as welcoming environments. Regardless of the problems entailed, good design and layout require natural as well as artificial light. Windowless rooms, whilst beneficial to hardware, are unacceptable environments for people.

Lighting

Each area should have glare-free lighting that meets acceptable architectural levels of foot-candles or lux (measured at tabletop height). Accommodations must be made for darkening viewing areas without disturbing other areas of the centre where work is to continue. Glare and reflection on computer monitors caused by inappropriate lighting fixtures should be avoided.

Climate

Heating, cooling, and ventilation should be adequate for both people and technology. Special attention must be paid to areas where photocopiers, dark rooms, and other production/repair areas are located, because of various hazards, including fumes.

Electricity

The basic rule is to put in as much as can be afforded and then more. Flexibility and access to power from any portion of the room(s) are necessary.

Acoustics

Carpeting is highly recommended, to keep noise levels down and allow a variety of activities to occur simultaneously, yet it can be the cause of unhealthy buildings. In such instances, wall and ceiling treatment may also be necessary to allow several groups and/or individuals to work simultaneously in the space.

Maintenance

Ongoing maintenance should be provided, including more than just taking care of daily-use debris. School holidays are usually the time that shelves are dusted and major cleaning tasks accomplished. Non-stop electrical power to servers and some workstations is required in automated environments.

Space

Library space is divided into discreet, but interrelated zones of activity. Care must be taken in designing the layout for the facility to consider traffic patterns, noise *vs.* quiet areas, leisure space areas, unobstructed sight lines, and appropriate adjacencies. The space should facilitate, not impede, the smooth operation of the library as well as its instructional programme. The layout can either positively or negatively affect the welcoming atmosphere inherent in a dynamic facility.

Main area

Flexibility, traffic patterns, and adjacencies should be the primary considerations. Provision should be made for adequate space for:
- circulation of resources along with the attendant storage requirements;
- computer workstations available for electronic or online research;
- the library 'card' catalogue, preferably electronic rather than print;
- the reference collection (adjacent to a group of computer workstations), with
- appropriate seating and tables;
- shelving that allows the logical storage of the general circulating collection of resources;

- periodical storage, either in hard copy, microforms, or provided through electronic or online access;
- Internet and www access;
- some comfortable seating for casual or leisure reading.

Class instructional area

In addition to the main area, the change in the emphasis of the information programme to a more formal instructional programme adds the need for an adjacent classroom or similar space that is well equipped with technology.

Small conference / student work areas

New teaching and learning strategies require students to work in teams or groups, to develop written reports, Power Point, Hyperstudio or other types of multimedia presentation. Space for groups to work productively as well as spread out without disturbing others is needed. Some libraries are building 'cabinets' for independent study where students may leave their resources and papers for an extended period of time with the assurance that they will not be disturbed.

Work / storage area / office

A work area, separated from the public areas needs to be provided for library staff as a secure place to work on new materials, update software, plan with teachers, *etc*. It would allow work in progress to remain undisturbed until they can return to it at a later time. The very nature of the library programme involves innumerable interruptions and distractions as students and faculty comes with their needs when they have a moment to do so. It should include space for the receipt and preparation of new acquisitions, a sink, work counter, and perhaps tables and chairs.

The work and storage areas should be readily accessible to a corridor for easy and quick deliveries of resources and the removal of packing materials. Unpacking and sorting books, checking invoices, materials processing and repair, hardware maintenance, typing, data entry, audio-visual production, photocopying and supplies all require work space and storage. The work area of the library is, after all, the warehouse management centre for the programme.

Technology space

While print collections may grow more slowly in the future, the space requirements for workstations, multimedia presentation areas, access to the Internet and www, printers and presentation hardware is ever expanding. Many primary source sites on the www are audio sites, causing complicated acoustical concerns. Head-end rooms, satellite (reception and transmission) and teaching areas all add space requirements to accommodate students and teachers.

Furnishing requirements – some suggested standards

Minimum space requirements (providing access by wheelchairs):
- 1.1m (42 in) between rows of shelves
- 1.5m (60 in) between rows of shelves and furniture involving seating
- 1.5m (60 in) between two tables or carrels with back-to-back seating

If a shelving run leads to a dead end, at least 1.5m (60 in) must be provided for a wheel chair to turn around. It is difficult for a wheel chair to back up more than two metres.

Shelving capacity

Type	Depth	Capacity per foot / 0.3m
Standard books	0.25 - 0.3m (10 -12 in)	8-10 books
Reference books	0.25 - 0.3m (10 -12 in)	6 books
Picture books	0.3m - (12 in) w/dividers	20 books
Periodicals	0.3m - (12 in) slanting	1 title
Disk recording	0.3m - (12 in) w/dividers	20 disks
Sound filmstrips (boxed)	0.3 - 0.4m (12 - 16 in)	5-6 boxes
Computer software	0.25 - 0.3m (10 - 12 in)	4 binders
Video cassettes	0.2 - 0.25m (8 - 10 in)	8-10 tapes

Shelving capacity - maximum heights

	Elementary	Secondary
Perimeter	1.5 - 1.8m (5 - 6ft)	1.8 - 2.1m (6 - 7ft)
Free-standing	1.1m (42in)	1.1m (42in) where visual control is needed 1.5 - 2.1m (5 - 7ft) where higher density storage is needed

NB All shelving should be firmly secured to a wall or floor in order to avoid the possibility of tipping over or shifting. It should be chosen with the age and height of the users in mind.

Free-standing single faced units are unsafe; similar double-faced units can be braced at the top for added stability.

Chairs and other seating - seat distance from floor

Elementary	0.36 - 0.43 m	(14 - 17 in)
Middle	0.4 - 0.46 m	(16 - 18 in)
High School	0.46 m	(18 in)

Tables and Carrels – maximum height of working surface

Elementary	0.63 - 0.71m (25 - 28 in)	keyboard height 0.65m/26 in
Middle	0.66 - 0.76m (26 - 30 in)	"
High School	0.71 - 0.76m (28 - 30 in)	"

Minimum clearance between chair seat and lowest edge of table top or of the 'skirt' (the brace under the table top around the perimeter of the table top – sometimes decorative, sometimes structural) 0.28m (11in)

Computer tables

0.76m (30 in) wide minimum - 0.99m (36 in) wide better
0.76m (30 in) deep minimum - hang CPU below desk top.
Remember to allow for printer, scanner, fax, *etc* space as well as the additional computer drops to put the peripherals on the network.

Chapter 7

Staff and Evaluation Guidelines

The librarian is a full member of the school's instructional team. In addition, because of the management and operational aspects of the library media centre programme and facilities, the librarian's responsibilities extend into the management arena. The inherent relationship that has developed between library information and new technologies requires new levels of technical expertise in order to provide the programme that today's students need to prepare them for the 21st century. These roles are totally interwoven in a vibrant, enthusiastic, responsive, optimally functioning library programme.

So, in addition to meeting the requirements of the teaching role and the traditional skills of the library world, the librarian must also possess specialised managerial and technological competencies.

The complexity of today's dynamic library media centre is often too extensive to be handled by one individual. Professional staff should be sought with complementary abilities in order to provide the full range of educational and informational services. Professional staff should also be supported by clerical assistance in order to devote as much time as possible to direct services to students and teachers. Performance evaluation should be based on the following five areas:
- planning
- organisation and management
- the teaching and learning process
- interpersonal relationships
- professional growth

These competencies provide a focus for goal setting early in the year. In addition, they define a more comprehensive and equitable assessment rubric for the complexity of today's library media programmes.

The Librarian's role:

In Planning

- Determines goals and objectives and implements them through the library media programme as an integral part of the instructional programme of the school.
- Develops policies which meet curricular, informational, and recreational needs of students.

- Establishes and applies criteria for decision-making concerning the advisability of locally produced resources as well as commercially available products.
- Applies the principles of research when supporting the development of new educational initiatives.
- Works with other related technical faculty and staff to develop a unified approach to the development of information systems within the school.

As Programme Manager

- Assesses the current state of the programme in terms of the school philosophy and goals.
- Prepares, justifies and administers the programme's budget;
- Establishes and administers processes and procedures for the efficient and economical selection, acquisition and evaluation of resources (books, media, online access, *etc*).
- Provides teaching and learning resources to enable teacher and student objectives in the curriculum.
- Arranges, uses, and develops a library facilities plan that best supports the various simultaneous uses of the centre, and particularly, the instructional programme.
- Builds and consults a collection of bibliographic aids and review tools for selection of resources.
- Establishes procedures for effective and efficient acquisition, processing, cataloguing, distribution and maintenance of resources (and equipment, if appropriate).
- Establishes an active public relations programme to keep faculty and students aware of new resources or programmes.
- Invites and accepts suggestions to improve the library media programme.
- Provides leadership and guidance, and encourages self-evaluation of the library media staff.
- Designs a programme to train and supervise student aides and volunteers, as appropriate.
- Implements policies and procedures for the management of the library programme.
- Co-ordinates the selection and acquisition of library resources (all instructional resources) and media.
- Evaluates the uses of emerging information technologies and their potential contribution to the educational programme.
- Develops and implements a plan of assessment and evaluation for the library programme.
- Keeps necessary records and statistics and writes reports of the status of the programme.
- Keeps the faculty aware of copyright laws and intellectual-freedom issues.

As teacher in the learning process

- Teaches information literacy and literary-appreciation skills to individuals and groups of students so that they may use the library with growing independence. Information literacy is defined as a three-part process:
    identification and access;
    evaluation;
    use of quality data/information to create new knowledge.
- Assists teachers and students in identifying, obtaining, and adapting materials to meet special needs.
- Recommends to teachers library resources and media in various formats which can help accomplish specific learning objectives.
- Promotes reading enjoyment and an appreciation of literature and information.
- Provides guidance in reading, listening, viewing, and speaking experiences for students and teachers.
- Plans learning activities and opportunities that will enable students to assume an increasing amount of responsibility for planning, undertaking and assessing their own learning.
- Designs instruction for students:
    emphasising the concepts and skills required in an information rich environment;
    identifying specific information sources and resources in a wide range of formats;
    evaluating what is found.
- Instructs and supervises teachers and students in developing creative and/or informative presentations in a variety of formats.
- Plans and conducts staff development opportunities for the library media staff and school faculty.
- Produces bibliographies, media materials, and other resources, which follow basic principles of instructional design for students and teachers.

In interpersonal relations and communications

- Recognises the components of the community structure and uses the specialised abilities, knowledge, and resources of people and institutions within the community to best advantage.
- Maintains an effective public-relations programme that communicates to all the vital contribution of the programme to learning.
- Participates in the evaluation and modification of teaching and learning designs as a member of the instructional team and in consultation with administrators.
- Serves on curriculum and other school committees.
- Maintains an atmosphere in the library that exudes a warm welcome to all students, faculty, and the parent community.

In professional development and as instructional consultant

- Keeps abreast of recent developments and trends in curriculum, teaching/learning strategies, instructional design, technology, and the library media profession in general.
- Sets yearly personal goals for growth and development.
- Reads extensively in the literature of the age groups served.
- Engages in self-evaluation to identify areas of need for continuing growth and professional development.
- Seeks professional growth opportunities, *eg* seminars, workshops, courses, training ... in areas of school librarianship, technology, and new directions impacting the teacher/learning process.

Ancillary staff

In addition to the librarian, support staff are often required to manage the day-to-day routines of the library operation, freeing up the professional's time for direct student and teacher contact. Schools address this situation in many ways, from a base level of trying to fill the need with volunteers, to adding non-professional staff for specific tasks, *eg* hardware maintenance, clerical support, media designer to work with students and faculty producing video or multimedia presentations.

Sample job descriptions for Head Librarian, Librarian, Aides, and Technical Support can be found in Appendix J.

Chapter 8

Programme Assessment Considerations

The activities of the library media programme are mirrored reflections of the curriculum as taught through a variety of strategies. While the library has its own information literacy curriculum, built around traditional organisational and informational skills, the learning process and application must come through regular and frequent classroom instructional activities. It is universally accepted that skills taught in a vacuum are neither retained, transferred, nor learned.

Therefore, the application of many of the skills required for an information literate student is a co-owned responsibility between the classroom and the information laboratories of the school, namely, the library and instructional technology programmes. Sometimes these are separate; other times a single unit. The required collaboration comes from two directions. Firstly the library continues to work with a wide variety of instructional technologies in addition to the computer. Secondly the knowledge of how the technology works, along with its standard software packages, needs to be augmented by an understanding of how information is organised and stored in an ever increasingly complex and anarchistic environment.

These two areas bring together the 'mechanical' aspects of the computer technology – how it works, how to use specific software tools to convey data, information, and ultimately knowledge – and the intellectual aspects of the information society in which data and information are no longer stored or presented in a linear fashion, but in an associative nature – how is it organised, indexed, accessed, evaluated, and ultimately understood. Both aspects of the information environment are absolutely essential for basic literacy in the lives of our students.

Assessment of the library programme can come in many forms – checklists of activities, evaluating planning and the resultant outcomes, the quality of the research students' produce, *etc*. The overriding characteristic of successful programmes is found in the integration and co-planning of instruction between the classroom and the library/information areas.

Some important indicators of the library programme's success are:
- The involvement of the librarian in the development of curriculum and implementation of a variety of instructional strategies
- The ease of access to people (human intervention), resources, and technology
- Time allocated for co-planning activities and team teaching with the librarian

- Development of increasingly complex research projects aimed at analysis of data rather than simply data gathering
- Identification of resources appropriate to the developmental level of the students
- The presence of a sufficiency of resources and ideas for the numbers of students requiring access
- The ability of students and faculty to deal with informational ambiguity, evaluation of sources and quality, understanding the who, what, how, and why some information is presented
- Awareness that information drives the format and that the format meets the learning styles of the students. While it is essential that the content be of the highest quality, the format must enhance not inhibit understanding and facilitate the transfer of the information to new situations. It appears that some children are better able to learn with different formats and it is their needs and not ours that must be paramount

The more recent modes of assessment based on competency documents, involvement with the teaching and learning process, and demonstrated performance attributes work well for the library programme.

The following list presents key questions upon which to base an assessment:
- Is there evidence of planning that reflects the philosophy and goals of the school and its instructional programme?
- Are policies and procedures in place, up-to-date and reflective of the school's instructional programme?
- Is there a collection development plan that enables the instructional programme and a variety of teaching strategies for teachers to meet individual needs?
- Are rules designed to invite people in rather than keep them out?
- Is the technology maintained? Reliable? Appropriate?
- Is the organisation of the facility conducive to a wide variety of simultaneous use? Are clerical tasks automated for efficiency?
- Is access to the collection via computer for ease of use by students and faculty?
- Is the library staff visible throughout the school? Part of the curriculum development teams? Continually growing professionally? Knowledgeable about current trends in the field and able to integrate them into the programme?
- Does the librarian use a variety of teaching strategies appropriate to developmental level and learning styles of students?
- Are resources readily accessible, well organised, up-to-date?
- Are instructional strategies appropriate for the developmental level of the students?

- Are resources selected for quality? Based on reviews? Are teachers involved in the selection process?
- Is self-assessment of programme and teaching routinely accomplished?
- Are services identified by faculty regularly incorporated into practice?
- Do all students and faculty have equal access to the programme and its supporting collection of resources and hardware?

Chapter 9

Public Relations, Display and Publicity

The library's support rests upon our success in developing resources and services that have meaning and importance to our users. Old images and impressions linger long after their viability. Today's libraries and information centres find themselves immersed in change, which leads to the assumption that others see this change, or are aware of how profound it is.

Public relations are an on-going, year-round effort. It involves not only telling others what you are doing, thinking, or planning but also eliciting from others what they see as their needs, desires and expectations. Developing a pro-active public relations programme draws on the elements of communication theory as well as the principles of public relations. Effective programmes are multi-faceted and involve a myriad of activities, some of which are mundane, others highly creative. The aim is to have everyone in the school community able to share the 'library story' accurately with others.

Librarians often argue that public relations take away valuable time from the 'real' work of the library or media centre. Yet, without a good public face, the library will be burdened by inaccurate perceptions that quickly become reality – at least in others' minds. It could be argued that a good public relations programme is simply an articulation of the many facets of the library programme and that being able to articulate this is the essential first step to understanding one's own relationship with the library programme.

Guidelines to consider in developing a good public relations programmes are:

Develop a plan

The process of planning creates an avenue for the programme to craft a clear picture of what its objectives are, and how they are to be achieved. A danger in planning is that it becomes the end, rather than the means to implementation. Exactly what is it that the programme wants others to know, recognise, take advantage of, focus attention on, *etc*? There may be so many facets to the programme that a clear focus may be lost trying to satisfy all needs at once. Planning will help prioritise competing interests into more manageable and achievable goals.

Understand the political pressures and implications

The library programme functions inside a school culture. Changing the culture is a difficult and long term process as is changing long held beliefs about what the library programme 'was when I was in school.' Recognise and acknowledge that there are unique pressures operating within each school and work with them rather than against them. Changes in curriculum, new knowledge of how children learn and how teachers teach, and general school reform efforts all influence the school culture. Communications should target the benefits to students and to the learning process – the ultimate beneficiaries of the programme's efforts.

Reflect on the timing of a public relations effort

The school year has a rhythm that builds as the year progresses. Understanding how the flow of time can affect the staff development or public relations efforts of the library is fundamental to its success or failure. For example, collection development efforts to involve a broad range of teachers and administrators cannot happen at the start of the academic year. Resources need to be in place by then. However, organising a series of information sessions or written communications aimed at specific collection enhancements that have just arrived would be welcome early in the year.

Form your relationships

Enlist the assistance of colleagues who believe what you believe to share the good news throughout the school community. These colleagues may be administrators, board members, teachers, parents, volunteers, student groups, sister agencies, other librarians or libraries. Be sure they are involved in carrying the positive images abroad to the wider educational community.

Delivery and content

Originality is often useful to open doors or catch attention, but the message is what you want to leave lingering on the mind of the audience. The message must be one that you can be absolutely sure you can deliver. Hollow promises and vague claims quickly label not only the current public relations effort, but will impede future efforts as well.

Define and identify a target audience

The audience will determine how the message is presented and how much information is bundled together at one time. While recent research has noted that adults need to hear something numerous times for it to be remembered, one cannot bore the audience repeatedly without losing them completely. You also want to help the audience understand what you hope they will do with the new found information. Different audiences require different approaches and techniques. Often the library programme has such a broad range of activities that it becomes tempting to overwhelm the audience with too much information at one time.

Assure that attainable goals are set and met

A fully functional public relations effort is very time consuming. Trying to 'do it all' will dilute its effectiveness. Return to the planning process to prioritise and sequence manageable goals that may last over a period of years.

Design a strategy

Determine what communication vehicles will be used to deliver the public relations programme. These can be both formal and informal communication modes and may range from the simplest newsletter or memo to the maintenance of a website.

Ask the 'hard' questions

Look at the strengths and weaknesses of the envisioned public relations efforts. If there are any controversial or weak areas, formulate and ask the 'hard' questions without waiting for an audience to point them out, often in a public forum. Be prepared to answer the 'naysayer' or sceptic without becoming defensive or unsure.

Evaluate, redefine, redevelop, move forward

Listen carefully to the school community to assess what works and what doesn't. Readjust, revise, and refine the programme on a regular basis. Solicit honest feedback, probe understandings, *etc* and make the adjustments necessary to stay on track.

A note of caution

Should a plan to survey your community emerge as a way of soliciting information from interested parties, be sure to only ask questions that are pertinent to the information being sought. Surveys often become 'fishing expeditions' asking irrelevant (even though interesting) questions. Asking questions that respondents would have no factual knowledge to inform their response often leads the respondent to reply with what they think the enquirer wants to hear.

If school librarians do not have a clear picture of who they are, their role within the educational community, their contribution to learning, and a solid command of the communication theory and practice – the tools of the trade – then they will not be able to project a strong, clear, positive image of their programmes to others.

Display and publicity

An adjunct to Public Relations is Display. The look of the library informs users about the resources and how they can be used. The library display projects an image to the school community and is invaluable in reinforcing the ethos and purpose of the library.

In *Display and Publicity for the School Library*, Dubber & Yendall, 1996, give a mnemonic, **AIDA**, that conveys how displays can be a powerful tool in developing an:

Awareness – of the school library amongst students and faculty
leading to an
Interest – in the resources of the library
and on to a
Desire – to find out more about the library and visit it
and so on to the
Action – of students and faculty using it

Displays are a means of assisting students to know and enjoy the library. Thought needs to be given to the display before and after creation. Ask students about the display – their usually honest opinions are a good evaluation source.

Think about the resources available for display – books, posters, student artwork and writing, photographs, and maps are just a small example.

Think about how the resources will be displayed and the materials to be used. For instance boxes can be covered with fabric or paper to create blocks for supporting books, different types of paper and card can be used for backgrounds.

Displays can be used to promote amongst others – authors, favourite books, themes, different cultures, festivals and new resources in the library. Books, magazines, cuttings and leaflets, posters, CD ROMs *etc* can be used to support the display.

The Library is not the only place to put a display – classrooms, the school hall, the main entrance and faculty lounge are areas where you can reach students, teachers, administrators, and parents.

Guiding and signing

As much a part of display is how library users find their way around the facility.
- Signs at the top of shelving bays that are readable from across the room
- Shelf guides that are movable for when the stock moves on the shelves
- Spine labels on information books

Signs should be clearly printed using an easily read typeface, in colour on a contrasting background. Do not use all capitals – these are harder to read than a mixture of upper and lower case.

A plan of the library is a useful aid to finding resources especially when there is a large library with island units, cupboards and filing cabinets.

Posters are a useful means of communicating necessary information such as an outline of the classification scheme, a reminder to students that the adults are there to help them. Students, as part of a library induction/orientation programme can create these.

Public relations tools

Materials and resources that keep the library in the eye of the school community are important.
- A library guide is useful to give to new students and staff – it could include names of staff and helpers, with photos if possible, opening hours, range of resources including information technology, number of books that can be borrowed, lending period, fines (if any), reservations, project loans *etc*. Remember that statements about library rules should be 'positive'. For instance you may take out a maximum of four books rather than you cannot take out more than four books.
- Bookmarks – either printed or 'home made' can remind users of the library – basic information can be included such as opening hours and staff names. The design can be a student project.
- Booklists – for each grade level; for vacation reading; ideas for parents; or relating to a particular author or class project.
- A library newsletter that involves students in its production can include details of new stock and book reviews.
- A library website, web pages and/or screen savers have a multiplicity of uses for the school library.

Reference

Dubber, Elizabeth & Yendall, David (1996). *Display and Publicity for the School Library*. SLA Guidelines. Swindon:School Library Association.

Appendices

Appendix A

Action Plan Recommendations

Editor's note

This summary of the 1987 research project's final report remains, in 1999, a guide for administrators, teachers, and librarians. The information world continues to evolve, sometimes in dramatic ways. Nevertheless, the suggestions contained herein remain viable even in today's world.

Carolyn Markuson 1999

The following information was drawn from a research study conducted in 1987. It was essentially for consumption in Europe by the schools. Its insights, however, remain and have much wider pertinence for heads, librarians and teachers. They are pointed and practical comments, which remain extremely useful. This introduction should, thus, be considered an integral part of the manual.

Gray Mattern 1988

Effective Libraries in International Schools Research Report

The research study upon which this manual is based was conducted in 1987. In addition to a survey and two ECIS Conference meetings, nine schools were visited – all were quite different. Some were large, some small; some had professional staff, others did not. The common theme that ran through all of the sites was a desire for a better quality school library programme, making a more substantial contribution to the school's educational offering. If the nine were a true sample of all the schools, they validated the research study findings, for their requests for assistance strongly supported and ran consistently parallel to the research study findings.

When comparing the difference between current practice and future aspirations, Heads indicated that they wished to see the most change/improvement in:
- the library as a dynamic intellectual force
- the library as a source of information, inspiration and recreation
- librarians involved in curriculum revision
- librarians as educational leaders in the schools

- school philosophy governing the library programme
- librarians fostering a love of reading

Librarians and heads agreed strongly on their mutual desire to see the following areas improved in the future:
- new teacher orientation
- students eager to use the library
- providing a link between curriculum areas and grade levels
- understanding teaching strategies and methodologies
- teachers and administrators providing role models in library use
- Singly, librarians were concerned most about improving resource selection
- a welcoming, stimulating library
- adjust services and collections to meet changes in student-body composition

All of these responses seem clearly to translate into a desire for a school library programme that is more inviting and exciting for students and teachers, embedded in the mainstream of the instructional process, and co-ordinated with classroom activities and experiences. The distance between desire and commitment, however, will spell the difference between achieving the goals or just giving lip service to the concept.

Heads consistently expressed a vision of the library as an instructional entity with an ongoing programme involving classroom integration. But in too many instances they are struggling to achieve this goal with non-professional staff (rarely accorded sufficient collegial status by the teaching faculty), or with a librarian provided with so little support staff that he/she must be all things – clerk, typist, cataloguer, circulation controller, story-teller – that is, teacher and library resource manager simultaneously. The 'librarian' is not involved in curriculum planning, and so the collection development is done in complete isolation by people with a minimal knowledge of children's literature and informational resources. Neither the library information skills nor the literary appreciation programme is connected with the classroom programme.

Placing non-professionals in peer relationships with teachers rarely works unless very unusual circumstances obtain. Non-professionals simply have little to contribute to a professional staff discussion about curriculum, strategies or methodologies. In other words, if the library is to be a vital extension of the classroom, the same calibre of professional teaching must be going on in both places.

Unfortunately, schools with a sophisticated philosophy of library service do not always have a professional librarian with the pedagogical background required to sustain the programme. This group of professional librarians well grounded in librarianship but not in teaching, needs to expand their skills to cope adequately with the new instructional thrust of school library programmes. In such situations, teachers also need to share the vision of the head for modern school library programmes.

In either of these alternatives, if the modern philosophy of school librarianship is embraced, the librarian's status in the school is not by itself sufficiently powerful to bring about change in the teaching strategies or methodologies of the classroom teacher. This power rests with the administrative leaders of the building. My impression was that American-trained librarians have more pedagogy in their training than their British or European counterparts. I also sensed, though did not have an opportunity to test, an impression that American-trained teachers used a central library more productively and more regularly in their classroom instruction than did British or other European-trained teachers. This does not imply one is any better than the other. It does mean, though, that if the philosophy of school librarianship based or modelled on the concept of the central importance of the school library/media centre is deemed appropriate, designing changes only at the library level will not be sufficient to bring about the desired results.

Change does not occur just because it is a wish. It must be clearly articulated, planned, and implemented in an orderly fashion. This requires vertical (heads, subject-area chairs and librarians) and horizontal (teacher and librarian) co-operation; consensus that the benefits are worth the effort; documentation of present conditions (a management manual, policies, procedures); a plan (multi-year); goals (where one wants to be); objectives (steps needed to be taken to achieve goals); and what needs to be done by or to each constituent group to achieve the ends desired. Needs assessment tools abound to determine 'where one is'; backplanning techniques (outcome planning) are most appropriate to determine 'where one wants to be' and to identify the crucial pieces of the programme that have to be in place to achieve the end. The advantage of the backplanning technique is that it focuses on performance indicators that clearly show that the goal is met, and then plans the steps that must be in place for that indicator to be present. The process is built from, but not tied to, past practices. It focuses on the final outcomes (three years ahead) and plans backwards from that.

Suggested avenues to explore – An improvement plan

There are several groups that must be involved and act in concert if change is to be achieved. Each has a unique contribution to make to the process of change. The absence of a key player may well render the planned change unattainable.

School administrators and leaders

(Heads and/or Principals)
- Provide consistent leadership and vision.
- Encourage appropriate staff-development-programme participation for librarians and classroom teachers.

- Choose the best (most creative, most respected) teachers to help plan and lead the change for the library programme.
- Involve the librarians on curriculum committees.
- Request the preparation of yearly goals and objectives for a) the managerial and organisational aspects of the programme, and b) the information literacy instructional programme.
- Require the library programme to develop a three-year plan of action with the assistance of a broadly based committee (many levels, many disciplines).
- Require the library to develop an operations manual (policy and procedures) to codify the operations, so that any new person coming on the job will be able to familiarise himself/herself as quickly as possible with its requirements and expectations and will not have to re-invent all the procedures.
- Recognise that the regular weekly classroom period of 'library' may in fact be negating efforts to integrate the library programme with the classroom. Look at more flexible scheduling plans. Teaching skills or literary appreciation in a vacuum is not good pedagogy (the Heads were in overwhelming agreement with this statement on the survey). In addition, younger students lack sufficient recall ability to be able to retain skills learned a week apart and not practised in between; skills taught without provision for regular practice are an exercise in futility. Flexible scheduling is a necessity, so that both short- and long-term involvement with a class is possible (at least above the Third-Grade level). Literacy appreciation is a major portion of the younger child's experience, and should take place in both the classroom and the library on at least a weekly basis.
- Involve library staff in discussions around literature-based reading programmes and writing-process activities. Both are natural connections with the elementary/junior school programme.
- Assure that the library is open every day the school is in session.
- Reduce 'obstacles' to the use of the library. If teachers encounter too may obstacles (or 'naysayers') in their attempts to connect with the library, they will find other ways of managing without it.
- In the absence of a trained librarian, put the best staff in the library. It is not a place for tired, burned-out staff. Provide some in-service or staff development to help them learn the intricacies of managing a circulating warehouse of resources, the importance of not re-inventing the wheel with new procedures, *etc*. Have them focus on learning the resources already there in some depth and working with teachers providing active services for children. Once such a scheme is in place and functioning well, then worry about new resources, technical services (cataloguing, classifying, *etc*). Use standard library tools (published bibliographies of 'Best Books', *etc*) and teacher suggestions to develop the collection until such time as a trained person is available.

- Hire people who bring as much talent to the required tasks as possible. Work with the librarian to develop job descriptions for positions. The old adage that no amount of supervision can correct a hiring mistake is absolutely true. People are most content when they are succeeding. Assign tasks to staff to take advantage of their best abilities.
- Keep library staff informed as to your expectations – and set them high. Counsel and help the staff to achieve these expectations. An active, vital library instructional programme has the same needs as an active, vital classroom.

Librarians

Collection development tends to follow training lines. Librarians schooled in America buy the major portion of their books from American jobbers; British-trained librarians do most or all of their purchasing from British book houses or jobbers. While there is a substantial amount of co-ordinated fiction publishing (simultaneous publication of the same work in America and Britain), only a few publishers are co-producing non-fiction for the marketplace. Publishers and jobbers are interested in making sales: they do not provide quality reviews upon which to base choices. Only reviewing tools do that. Top choice tools in the print world are *The School Librarian* (British) and *School Library Journal* or *Booklist* (American). These publications should be used by professionals as the primary selection tools for collection development.

[Please see **Collection Development** Appendix D for recent developments in this area. CM]

- Keep up with current training. Seek summer institutes and, if applicable, teaching skills necessary to provide the kind of library the school is seeking. Minimise the clerical work done in-house. Buy the cataloguing wherever possible. Use reviews to purchase books, including published bibliographies. Hoard your time for student/teacher interaction and view with suspicion any activity that tears you away from that.
- Develop a three-year or five-year plan with the assistance of an advisory committee, broadly representative of many disciplines. Set yearly goals following the suggestion in the administrators' remarks.
- Set priorities for curriculum planning/revision participation, if unable to participate in it all. For example, writing-process and literature-based reading programmes may be where you begin to work with curriculum, moving on to other areas in a cycle. It may be unrealistic to assume you are part of every curriculum team every year. In those times where consistent involvement is not possible, make regular contact with department leaders to learn what is happening.
- Make yourself available to staff – at lunch, at coffee, as much as possible. Enormous amounts of information and interaction occur informally around chance meetings. If you are always in the library,

those chances never come. If it is not possible for you to be out and about, find a way to get teachers in – coffee, photocopier, *etc*.
- If trained as a teacher, but not as a librarian, seek courses or read extensively in library professional literature. Include a knowledge base about how technology and new formats of information are organised, and how best to use them to the student's advantage.
- If trained as a librarian but not as a teacher, expand your knowledge of child development, teaching strategies, learning styles and learning theory, and on current theories of how children learn (cognitive psychology). Learn what authentic assessment, constructivist classrooms, active learning, portfolio assessments, *etc* mean and how they can be enhanced through the library programme.
- Skills instruction needs to be embedded in context that comes from the classroom. Make the context happen; don't teach the skills in a vacuum. Remember that reading is also a skill that requires practice. The busy classroom does not allow time for sufficient practice (research tell us that the average time spent reading in a classroom is under six minutes per day!). Also recognise that learning to decode (reading instruction) and literature appreciation (loving to read) are two distinct but entwined parts of a whole.
- The librarian's 'homework' is different from that of the teacher. There are no papers to correct, parent conferences, or grades. But there are lesson plans, preparation, and reading required for good job performance! One cannot enthusiastically recommend books, computer software, or other resources to children with only a cursory overview, or an unplanned, off-the-top-of-one's-head lesson.

Teachers

- Be involved with the programme the library is working to initiate.
- Participate on advisory committees.
- Recognise that, in an information age, the textbook becomes more inadequate than ever, students must have the opportunity to learn how to find information as well as be given it.
- Involve the librarian in your classrooms – doing booktalks, skills instruction, readings, consulting on assignments, co-teaching, *etc*.
- Consult with the librarian when planning assignments and new activities in your subject area.
- Share with the librarian information about students – how the brightest can be challenged, the middle encouraged to practise, the slowest to find and use appropriate resources and move upwards.
- Encourage enquiry, multiple opinions, and synthesis of information. Most resources provide data and information, which students need to coupled with thoughtful analysis, in order to create new knowledge – and ultimately wisdom!
- Recognise that process is as important as product. Involve the librarian

in the evaluation of the process of seeking, gathering, and synthesising information. Libraries as we knew them – as repositories of limited formats of information – have ceased to exist. However, information continues to expand. As it does so, it becomes increasingly more complex for an individual to find the specific pieces needed (an experience we have had using the www). Responses in the research study unanimously agreed that this skill is a basic necessity for today's (and tomorrow's) children.

Appendix B

Standards & Guidelines

Supporting IB programmes

The International Baccalaureate Organisation currently offers Diploma and Certificate programmes, a Middle Years Programme, and a Primary Years Programme. All materials and information are sent to schools via the IB co-ordinator, so it is essential that the librarian makes regular contact with the co-ordinator, to ensure that s/he sees all relevant documents. Materials are normally sent only in single copies, it is expensive to buy extra copies, and the co-ordinator normally duplicates materials for individual teachers. The librarian should make a point of looking at new materials, and copying bibliographies and any other information relevant to the library programme. Two copies of the journal IB World are sent to all IB schools, so one copy can be kept in the library.

Regular workshops are held in most regions for librarians in IB schools, as well as for all subjects. These informative gatherings become part of the staff development and on-going learning of the librarian.

Diploma and Certificate programmes

The IBO publishes syllabi and sets exams, but does not specify teaching methods or materials to be used. However, teachers' guides and other materials are published for each subject, and many of these contain useful bibliographies. It can be helpful to ask teachers for bibliographies when they come back from subject courses, as they often get useful materials, which they may not think to share with the librarian. The librarian needs to know which courses are being taught in his/her school, and which options, where these exist. S/he then needs to work with teachers to identify suitable resources. Diploma students are required to write an Extended Essay on a subject of their choice. Librarians in non-English speaking countries are advised to cultivate relations with any local library with an English language collection (*eg*, local colleges, British Council, *etc*) so that students have a local source beyond the school library.

Middle Years and Primary Years programmes

The MYP and PYP concentrate more on how students learn than on what they learn, and hence, there is a more obvious role for the librarian in the teaching of research and information skills. The librarian in schools undertaking MYP and/or PYP should become involved from the planning stages, as the library has a vital role and contribution to make – indeed, it should be central to the delivery of these programmes. Libraries are required to reach certain standards before schools are accepted into the programmes.

Full information on all programmes can be obtained from the IBO. To effectively support IB programmes, schools should aim for the mature level of library services, as previously outlined in this guide.

IB Library Guidelines

As the International Baccalaureate Organisation does not dictate teaching methods and materials, neither does it lay down requirements for school libraries. These guidelines have been drawn up by the IBO Librarians Committee in response to requests from teachers and librarians to advise on building libraries to support the IBO Diploma and Middle Years programmes, and are intended only as suggestions for good practice. Existing published guidelines for school libraries have been relied on, and the authors of these are acknowledged, in producing this document.

Ideally, students in the IB Diploma and Middle Years programmes need access to a well-stocked library providing a range of print and non-print materials, with a professional librarian, so that they can read beyond what is taught in the classroom, and learn and practice research and information-handling skills.

The IBO Annual Report for 1993-94 pointed out that:
- knowledge is expanding in volume at an almost unmanageable pace
- there are now many more ways of accessing this knowledge
- the shelf-life of much of this body of knowledge is becoming shorter.

Therefore we need to concentrate as much on teaching how, as on teaching what, and on giving students the skills to be lifelong self-directed learners.

As one of the aims of the IBO Diploma programme is preparation for higher education, we need to equip students with the necessary skills to make effective use of the large automated libraries most of them eventually be required to use.

There are a number of published guides and standards, which go into detail about library provision and services, and we refer schools to these. We recognise that schools offering the IB Diploma and/or Middle Years programmes vary greatly in the existing standards of their libraries, and in the level of funding available, and these guides have been chosen with this diversity in mind.

Baird, Nicola (1994) *Setting Up and Running a School Library* (London: Heinemann). This was written with the co-operation of Voluntary Service Overseas, and as a practical guide for setting up school libraries where funds are limited and there is no professional librarian.

Carrol, Frances (1988) *Guidelines for School Libraries* (Washington, DC: IFLA Section of School Librarians and Association for Educational Communications and Technology. American Library Association).

It is recognised that librarians working in European schools have selected the above titles, and there are probably titles available in other regions, which are of equal value. *IB information obtained from the website <www.ibo.org>*

Common Goals for Student Learning

Source: *The National Study of School Evaluation and The Alliance for Curriculum Reform* (1996), Washington, DC

Learning to learn

Gather and use information effectively
Reflect on and assess their learning
Demonstrate adaptability and flexibility
Effectively use goal setting and planning skills (*eg* self-management skills, time management, *etc*)
Demonstrate perseverance and self-discipline

Expanding and integrating knowledge

Make explicit connections within and across areas of learning based upon an understanding of the disciplines
Use existing knowledge to expand understanding or develop new knowledge
Gain disciplinary knowledge and use multi-disciplinary connections in the course of solving authentic problems

Communication skills

Communicate with clarity, purpose, and understanding of audience
Use a wide range of communication forms effectively and appropriately (*eg* oral, written, artistic, graphic, *etc*)
Recognise, analyse, and evaluate various forms of communication

Thinking and reasoning

Critical Thinking, Problem Solving, and Creative Thinking
Analyse, synthesise, and draw inferences from observations and other data to define and solve problems

Construct and justify arguments using logic and evidence appropriate to the context and audience
Assess, critique, and refine their problem-solving strategies
Explore various paths, use multiple strategies, and take considered risks in solving problems and in creative expression
Reflect on her/his own pattern of perception and learning

Interpersonal skills

Work with others in a variety of situations to set and achieve goals.
Manage and evaluate their behaviour as individuals and as group members
Deal effectively and tolerantly with diverse opinions and beliefs
Negotiate effectively to achieve goals

Personal and social responsibility

Personal Responsibility
    Take responsibility for personal actions
    Strive for excellence; demonstrate commitment to quality
    Act ethically (*eg* demonstrate honesty, fairness, integrity, *etc*)
    Respect self and others
Social Responsibility
    Understand and appreciate the diversity and interdependence of all people
    Act as responsible citizens of the community, state, and nation
    Develop responsibility for global and environmental issues.

Information literacy standards for student learning

Source: *Information Power: Building Partnerships for Learning* (1998) Chicago, IL: American Association of School Librarians and the Association for Education and Communication Technology.

Information literacy standards

I The student who is information literate accesses information efficiently and effectively.

   Indicators

    1 Recognises the need for information
    2 Recognises that accurate and comprehensive information is the basis for intelligent decision making
    3 Formulates questions based on information needs
    4 Identifies a variety of potential sources of information
    5 Develops and uses successful strategies for locating information

II The student who evaluates information critically and competently

Indicators

1. Determines accuracy, relevance, and comprehensiveness
2. Distinguishes among fact, point of view, and opinion
3. Identifies inaccurate and misleading information
4. Selects information appropriate to the problem or question at hand

III The student who uses information accurately and creatively

Indicators

1. Organises information for practical application
2. Integrates new information into one's own knowledge
3. Applies information in critical thinking and problem solving
4. Produces and communicates information and ideas in appropriate formats

Independent learning standards

IV The student who is an independent learner is information literate and pursues information related to personal interests.

Indicators

1. Seeks information related to various dimensions of personal well being, such as career interests, community involvement, health matters, and recreational pursuits
2. Designs, develops, and evaluates information products and solutions related to personal interests

V The student who appreciates literature and other creative expressions of information

Indicators

1. Is a competent and self-motivated reader
2. Derives meaning from information presented creatively in a variety of formats
3. Develops creative products in a variety of formats

VI The student who strives for excellence in information seeking and knowledge generation

Indicators

1. Assesses the quality of the process and products of personal information seeking
2. Devises strategies for revising, improving, and updating self-generated knowledge

Social responsibility standards

VII The student who contributes positively to the learning community and to society is information literate and recognises the importance of information to a democratic society

Indicators

1. Seeks information from diverse sources, contexts, disciplines, and cultures
2. Respects the principle of equitable access to information

VIII The student who practices ethical behaviour in regard to information and information technology

Indicators

1. Respects the principles of intellectual freedom
2. Respects intellectual property rights
3. Uses information technology responsibly

IX The student who participates effectively in groups to pursue and generate information.

Indicators

1. Shares knowledge and information with others
2. Respects others' ideas and backgrounds and acknowledges their contrbutions
3. Collaborates with others, both in person and through technologies, to identify information problems and to seek their solutions.

Appendix C

Information Literacy Research Models

Information skills sequences

There are many ways to organize and present information literacy skills. The following models offer examples of scope as well as methods of organization. Customizing the list to the school learning environment will help a library instruction programme to have realistic goals and optimize opportunities for interaction with academic areas.

Model 1: Elementary School Level

This model concentrates on building a strong programme in basic skills in a low-tech environment. Standards are aimed at building awareness of information sources and appreciation for reading and exploring for learners in grades K-3.

Library citizenship standards

The student will
1. understand the concept of the library as a source of reading pleasure and intellectual exploration
2. understand the role of the librarian as a resource to information and reading
3. exhibit appropriate library behaviour
4. exhibit proper care and handling of library materials

Library usage standards

The student will
5. understand procedures for checking out and returning library materials
6. be able to return library materials to their proper places
7. understand the prefixes on call numbers
8. locate materials for his/her reading level
9. know the difference between fiction and non-fiction
10. understand the arrangement of materials by the Dewey Decimal System
11. locate a book in the library catalog by title and author

Library resources standards

The student will
12   recognize simple parts of a book
13   know the difference between a book and a magazine
14   use illustrated reference books (*eg*, atlases, encyclopedias, dictionaries)
15   know the range of formats of library materials
16   recognize award winning children's authors and their works

Application of library skills standards

The student will
17   re-tell a story s/he has read
18   recognize relevant information found in a resource
19   summarize, orally and in writing, what s/he has learned from a resource
20   paraphrase what s/he has read

Model 2: Middle High School Level

This model supports a highly interactive library programme in a high tech environment. Skills categories are tailored to integrate the skills with academics; standards are selected to focus on what learners need to know and be able to do in order to apply information skills in the context of their academic subjects and in the context of the high tech environment.

Personal management skills

The student will
1   analyse and break down tasks, assignments
2   set goals
3   complete monthly calendar, organise long term assignments
4   record assignments in planner
5   manage time effectively
6   participate gainfully in co-operative work
7   follow proper procedures for use of the computer lab
8   understand the role of the library as a resource centre
9   know library procedures, policies, services
10   care for borrowed materials and exhibit proper library conduct
11   know the layout and organization of the library
12   be aware of the range of library services
13   understand the role of the library in a free society
14   know ethical, legal responsibilities for reproduction of library materials

15 understand the importance of using resources independently
16 know how to care for a computer disk, directories and files

Study skills standards

The student will
17 use SQ3R
18 be aware of specific study skills for other content areas
19 be able to use scanning and skimming
20 read with a purpose and for meaning
21 use the writing process
22 write for specific purposes
23 write for specific audiences
24 use active listening and schemata
25 use questions for clarification
26 apply test taking strategies
27 use long term preparation for a test
28 'read' an exam
29 manage test anxiety
30 be aware of learning style
31 apply memorising techniques
32 take 'shopping list' notes
33 classify and categorise information
34 imagine questions
35 identify key words

Information retrieval skills standards

The student will
36 identify, locate, retrieve and use reference materials
37 locate, retrieve and use information stored on microfiche
38 use electronic systems on CD-ROM and discs to access information
39 differentiate between on-line and internal networks and databases
40 understand the purpose and function of the Dewey Decimal System
41 execute subject, title and author searches in the library catalogue
42 execute a key word search using one term
43 execute a multiple key word search using Boolean logic
44 compile a list of key words, or search terms
45 select, evaluate, and retrieve materials using the library catalogue
46 identify and locate the works of award winning authors

Research skills standards

The student will
47 take notes from the chalk board
48 take notes during oral presentations

49 take notes from viewing audio-visual presentations
50 take notes from print and electronic references
51 write an outline from notes
52 create a mind map from notes
53 ask useful literal and exploratory questions from notes
54 classify and analyse information
55 evaluate information, separating the relevant from irrelevant
56 expand notes into a written report
57 recognise scholarship and avoid plagiarism
58 write a bibliography using an acceptable format
59 transform information and present it in diverse formats
60 develop a research question
61 write a research proposal
62 cite sources using direct quotation
63 distinguish between hard and soft data
64 define and locate parts of a book or electronic source
65 evaluate sources used in research

Computer skills standards

The student will
66 know how to use basic computer hardware
67 identify daily applications of computers in society
68 recognise the impact of computers on daily life
69 use appropriate computer vocabulary
70 demonstrate familiarity with basic WINDOWS commands
71 type at the rate of 20-30 wpm
72 set up, format and edit and print a word processed document
73 set up a database using field names and records
74 sort a database
75 query a database
76 print reports from a database
77 set up a spreadsheet using columns and rows
78 use formulas to do calculations in a spreadsheet
79 create charts from spreadsheets
80 apply data logging techniques to collect data
81 apply problem solving techniques to complete simulations
82 retrieve clip art into a word processing document
83 use Drawing, Paint Brush, Power Point or other appropriate applications
84 create home pages using html

Support Materials for Research Process Models

The Research Proposal form

Research Question	Sub Questions a. b. c.
Key Words/Terms 1. 2. 3. 4. 5.	Definitions of Key Words/Terms 1. 2. 3. 4. 5.
Submitted by _____ Student	Approved by _____ _____ Advisor/Teacher Date
Working Bibliography: Titles	What do I need to know to find them again? (*eg*, Call number, Internet address)
Submitted by: _____ Student	Approved by: _____ _____ Advisor/Teacher Date

The Research Proposal, How to do it

1 Formulate the research question or research statement. (What are you curious about?)
   - Is the question too broad or too narrow?
   - Can the question be broken down into sub-questions or sub-divisions? What are they?
   - What are the key words in the question and sub-questions?
   - Can I find information?

2 Plan the research design
   - Build a rationale for your study. (Why is it important?)
   - Choose resources for collecting data/information
   - Choose methods of analysing data/information

3 Key Words
Record at least five words and/or terms that are critical to your research. Use the key words to:
   - formulate the research question
   - search for information
   - select sources for note-taking
   - take notes
   - write the essay (introduction, body, conclusion)

4 Working Bibliography
Include the titles and location information for books, magazines, newspapers, CD-ROMs, Internet, on-line sources, people, and primary sources. This is a preliminary list of sources of information that you think will be useful or that you need to read for background to help formulate your research question.

Example of a Proposal

Research Question	Sub Questions
Will the computer change the way we are schooled?	a What are the positive and negative aspects of computers in learning? b Could current problems in teaching be solved by computers? c Will schools become obsolete?
Key Words/Terms 1 Information superhighway 2 E-mail 3 Network 4 Virtual reality 5 Multimedia	**Definitions of Key Words/Terms** 1 A vast network of shared information through computer, television, satellite. 2 Messages sent electronically between computers via a computer network. 3 A system of interconnected equipment such as telephones and computers that can communicate with each other. 4 Computer or other electronic software that allows the user to experience asimulated environment. 5 The incorporation of many types of media such as graphics, text, audio, and video into one resource.
Research Design The essay will be written in a compare and contrast form. The advantages and disadvantages of computers in learning will be discussed to establish the conclusion to the research question.	**Data Collection Methods** 1 Notes from secondary sources 2 Interviews with teachers 3 Questionnaires to students **Methods of Analysis** 1 The pros and cons of computers with regard to learning 2 Problem solving: relating learning/teaching problems to the potential of computers.
Working Bibliography Titles *The Road Ahead* *The Virtual School* *The Children's Machine* *Internet and World Wide Web* *The Computer Revolution in Education*	**What do I need to know to find them again?** e.g Call number, Internet address 001 GAT http://www.virtualschool.yaleuniv.edu PRO 371.3 PAP 001 KEN *Time,* June 28, 1996, p.19

Student Evaluation of the Project

Project evaluation, 10th Grade research paper

Here is your chance to grade us! What did you think of the project? Assign a number to each statement. 4 is the highest rating that indicates you agree and 1 is the lowest score that indicates your disagreement.

1   The timelines were reasonable
        1   2   3   4

2   Instructions were clear
        1   2   3   4

3   Library resources were adequate
        1   2   3   4

4   The grading system was fair
        1   2   3   4

5   The Bibliography Charts were helpful
        1   2   3   4

6   The Key word list was helpful
        1   2   3   4

7   I feel prepared for the Extended Essay
        1   2   3   4

8   Forming a research question and sub-questions was helpful
        1   2   3   4

9   I felt well prepared to search for information
        1   2   3   4

10   I could get help when I needed it
        1   2   3   4

11   I liked the idea of using two methods of data collection
        1   2   3   4

12   I liked the idea of using two methods of analysis
        1   2   3   4

Project evaluation – what do you think?

1. What were the best aspects of this project?

2. What would you change?

3. What was the most difficult task you had? Why was it difficult?

4. How was this research assignment different from the way you have done research in the past?

5. What did you learn that will help you do your Extended Essay next year?

6. Do you think it was worth the class time allotted? Why?

7. Other comments?

References

Ausubel, D P (1963). *The Psychology of Meaningful Verbal Learning*. New York: Grune and Stratton.

Breivik, P (1985). *Putting libraries back in the information society*. American Libraries, 16 (10), p723.

Callison, D (1986). School library media programs and free inquiry learning. *School Library Journal*, 32 (6), p20-24.

Collins, A, & Dana, T M (1993). Using portfolios with middle grade students. *Middle School Journal*, 25 (2), p14-19.

Dana, TM, & Tippins, D J (1993). Alternative assessments for middle school learners. *Middle School Journal*, 25 (2), p3-5.

Davis S J (1994). Teaching practices that encourage or eliminate student plagiarism. *Middle School Journal*, 25 (3), p55-58.

Eisenberg, M & Brown, M (1992). Current research. *School Library Media Quarterly*, 21(3).

Irving, A (1981). *Information Skills in the Secondary Curriculum*. London: Methuen Educational.

Irving, A (1985). *Study and Information Skills across the Curriculum*. Portsmouth: Heinemann.

Jacobs, H H (1997). *Designing Performance Based Assessment, Rubrics, and Feedback Systems*. Paper presented at the meeting of the European Council of International Schools, The Hague, Netherlands, November.

Kuhlthau, C C (1984). *The Library Research Process: Case Studies and Interventions with High School Seniors in Advanced Placement English Classes Using Kelly's Theory of Constructs*. Unpublished doctoral dissertation, Rutger's University, New Jersey.

Kuhlthau, C C (1987). An emerging theory of library instruction. *School Library Media Quarterly*, 16 (1), p23-28.

Kuhlthau, C C (1988). *The Information Search Process of High, Middle and Low Achieving High School Seniors*. Paper presented at the meeting of the Research Forum of the American Association of School Librarians, New Orleans, LA.

Loertscher, D V (1996). President's Column. *School Library Media Quarterly*, 24 (4), p192.

Mancall, J C, Aaron, S L, & Walker, S A (1986). Educating students to think: The role of the school library media program. *School Library Media Quarterly*, 15 (1), p18-27.

Powell, J C (1993). What does it mean to have authentic assessment? *Middle School Journal*, 25(2), p36-42.

Sheingold, K (1987). Keeping children's knowledge alive through inquiry. *School Library Media Quarterly*, 15 (2), 80-85.

Soodak, L C & Martin-Kniep, G O (1994). Authentic Assessment and Curriculum Integration: Natural Partners in Need of Thoughtful Policy. *Educational Policy*, 8 (2), p183-201.

Wiggins, G (1992). Creating tests worth taking. *Educational Leadership*, 48 (8), p 26-33.

Appendix D

Collection Development & Management

Selection and collection development resources

The following is a list of resources in print that can inform the selection process. It provides lists of quality resources that are available for libraries. Some include reviews of current or recent publications, while others provide comprehensive lists of previously recommended titles. Many include audio-visual (cassettes, videos, CD-ROMs, *etc*) resources for purchase consideration. In addition, many include articles on state of the art activities, management techniques, *etc* for the library.

In addition, the electronic world has once again come to our assistance. Many of the print resources listed in the bibliography are available on the www, albeit in limited coverage. These, coupled with the advent of web-based book stores has also given us a means to identify quickly what is in print (print and media in some cases), and retail costs. These www sites, such as Amazon.com <http://www.amazon.com> or Barnes and Noble.com <http://www.barnesandnoble.com> provide subject access, and many reviews. Also, large library vendors are putting their catalogues on the web, such as Follett's Titlewave. It is worth noting that popular press reviews, aimed at the home market, may not be a valid assessment for a school setting. Nonetheless, these new avenues allow us to quickly identify what is available on the topics we are seeking and make 'blind' purchasing unnecessary.

When coupled with www library catalogues, bookstores' lists can be authenticated against a known major (or known quality) library's holdings. For non-professionals making selection decisions, this provides an additional validation of a particular title. It offers an opportunity to use our library network to help us make sound decisions. An example of how this works would be a search for books on the Wampanoag Indians of Southeastern Massachusetts. The www list obtained shows 44 titles at the appropriate age level, many without reviews. What to do? Well, a check of the web-based 'card' catalogue for the Brookline Public Library, an excellent local library, finds several titles from the list have been included in their children's collection – a validation of quality. The international network of librarians and libraries can (will in the future) be able to offer similar assistance.

Bibliography of print selection and deselection tools

100 best books: the pick of the paperback stories for children from toddlers to teenagers. London: Young Book Trust. (Annual).

* *Book Report.* Linworth Publishing, Inc. 480 East Wilson Bridge Rd, Suite 1, Worthington, OH 43085. USA.

Bookbird. *Literature for Children and Young People, News from All Over the World, Recommendations for Translations,* Lucia Binder Knud-Eigil Hauberg-Tychsen, Mayerhofgasse 6, A-1040 Vienna, Austria.

Booklinks. American Library Association, 50 E Huron Street, Chicago, IL 60611, USA.

* *Booklist.* American Library Association, 50 E Huron Street, Chicago, IL 60611, USA.

Doll, Carol A & Petrick Barron, Pamela (1991). *Collection analysis for the school library media center : a practical approach.* Chicago: American Library Association.

Elementary School Library Collection. 21st ed (1998). Williamsport, PA: Brodart, USA.

* *Emergency Librarian.* Box 34069, Department 284, Seattle, WA 98124, USA.

Ho, May Lein & David Loertscher (1988). Collection mapping: the research. In: David V Loertscher (ed). *Measures of excellence for school library media centres.* Pp22-39. Englewood, CO: Libraries Unlimited.

* *Horn Book.* Horn Book, Inc, Suite 1000, 11 Beacon St., Boston, MA 02108, USA.

* *Library Talk.* Linworth Publishing, Inc 480 East Wilson Bridge Rd., Suite 1, Worthington, OH 43085, USA.

Lima CW (1998) *A to Zoo: Subject Access to Children's Picture Books.* 5th edition. NY: Bowker.

MultiCultural Review. 88 Post Road, P. O. Box 5007, Westport, CT 06881, USA.

* *Multimedia Schools.* Online Inc, 462 Danbury Road, Wilton, CT 06897, USA.

* *The School Librarian.* School Library Association, Liden Library, Barrington Close, Liden, Swindon, Wilts. SN3 6HF, UK.

* *School Library Journal.* RR Bowker, New Providence, NJ 07974, USA.

* *Signal.* Thimble Press, Lockwood, South Woodchester, Stroud, Glos. GS5 5EQ, UK.

Slote, Stanley J (1997) *Weeding library collections : library weeding methods,* 3rd ed. Englewood, CO: Libraries Unlimited.

Van Orden, P.(1995) *The Collection Program in Elementary and Middle Schools.* 2nd ed. Littleton, CO: Libraries Unlimited.

*Key professional journals – reviewing tools useful for selection

Keeping the collection relevant – deselection

A good deal of time is spent selecting materials for the library programme of services. The selection process is guided by the selection policy, which normally includes a section on deselection, or weeding. School libraries are for the most part reflections of the instructional programme of the school, and not archival storage facilities.

While some recreational reading is both necessary and desirable, today's collections are carefully 'mapped' to the curriculum – the topics and objectives of the instructional programme. As the curriculum and teaching strategies change, so does the emphasis and composition of the collection. New courses are added, other courses are eliminated; still others may be changed or moved to a different plane, *eg* combined into interdisciplinary or thematic experiences. All of these changes in curriculum should be reflected in the collection.

Many faculty and administrators mistakenly assume that once a resource is purchased, it is viable forever. This is a more dangerously incorrect assumption than it has ever been with today's rapidly changing information landscape. We all know that young children do not bring an adult experiential background to their work. When they see a statement 'Someday we will land on the moon', or 'The principal [always 'he'] runs the schools like your mother runs the house,' they have no experiential knowledge that could refute what they see in print. As the information world has moved into a robust electronic world, the format of the information also becomes important. Students prefer to work with newer technologies; older electronic resources do not run on newer hardware.

In addition, shelves full of titles with misinformation or disinformation make it difficult for students to select those items that would meet their needs. Research studies have shown that only the adults reflect nostalgically on their 'old' readings. Students do not choose to read stories that are distractingly illustrated with out-dated images. In fact, with the exception of classics (both contemporary and traditional ones) fiction resources older than seven to eight years are seldom selected for reading even with the intervention of an energetic and enthusiastic recommendation. Science, medicine, political entities, world economies, *etc* continue to change with ever-increasing speed over time. The collection must not reflect the inaccuracies of the past but provide today's students with an accurate picture of the world of today. Their mental models require that they learn accurate, up-to-date information.

Discarded materials should not be used to form the crux of classroom collections. While encyclopedias can remain viable for five to ten years in some topic areas, they quickly become dated in many others. Quick access should be weighed against the inaccurate information students may acquire in the process.

Hardware presents other problems. Older hardware, particularly computer hardware, will not run newer software or runs it so poorly that it cannot be effectively used. While it occasionally may be usable on an individual basis or for a particular purpose, once the care and maintenance becomes excessive, or its non-use outweighs its viable use, it should be retired permanently.

Shelving and storage space is always at a premium in schools. To clutter such storage with permanent shelf-sitters costs the school valuable space.

Some criteria upon which to make deselection decisions are
- badly out-of-date information
- misleading information
- poorly-written resources (often these creep into recreational reading collections)
- resources on topics no longer in the curriculum need to be reviewed
- unnecessary duplicates
- resources that portray racism, stereotyping, or scapegoating
- torn or tattered resources (perhaps with a replacement in mind)
- resources not used for a five to seven year period
- audiovisuals that are no longer audible (poor sound) or have poor quality visuals
- hardware that continually destroys software or malfunctions
- materials no longer listed in standard catalogues or indexes
- better formats now available

What can be done with these resources? Unfortunately, very little. If they remain viable because of a shift in curriculum, perhaps another repository would be possible. However, if they are deemed inappropriate for our children, they should simply be discarded, not redeployed.

Evaluation of various formats

The core value of any resource is the quality of the information contained within. Without this, all of the other attributes become irrelevant. Print materials have a publisher and presumably an editor behind their products; nonprint and www materials often do not have this advantage.

Computer-based learning software requires careful scrutiny as it is easy to get caught up in the 'glitz' and forget that the software must first contribute to the educational programme. Many popular edutainment and educational software packages fail to meet the test of quality, have major pedagogical flaws, or have simply taken old materials (*eg* 1950's filmstrips) and put them onto a new format (with a new copyright!). Industry reports claim that the CDROM market has yet to turn a profit for the companies involved in developing and marketing this format. Yet, as a means of accessing complex programs (such as the Microsoft Office application) they provide great benefit over stacks of 3.5" floppy disks.

Primary attributes

Authenticity of information
Depth / breadth of information
Relationship of content to curriculum needs
Appropriate to the intended audience and grade level
Appropriate and accurate language and terminology
Illustrations and graphics enhance and extend text

Technical attributes

Presentation of the information is appropriate to the medium
Audio is clear and easily understood
Includes convenient and versatile print routines
Works on existing hardware
Adheres to principles of instructional design
Comes with an uninstall programme
Doesn't automatically overwrite existing software, plug-ins, *etc*
Loads quickly and efficiently
Links are logically grouped

General attributes

Currency of information / regularly updated website
Screen design facilitates ease of use (*eg*, intuitive icons)
Cross-referenced access
Key word as well as subject access
Signed articles or sections
Includes a help line phone number (free?)
Includes good documentation
Easy to install
Stimulates the imagination
Interactivity pedagogically extends the new knowledge just learned
Correct spelling and grammar use

IB union list of periodicals – summary

The top 100

Based on an I B schools questionnaire distributed in 1995. Some 3800 titles were recorded, five or more schools held 425 titles.
* Indicates most used research periodicals in US High Schools.

The IB list of 100 most commonly held titles:

No. Schools	Title
131	*National Geographic
111	*Time
102	*Newsweek
97	*Scientific American
80	*Sports Illustrated
76	Discover
69	Seventeen
66	*Science News
66	*US News & World Report
63	Popular Science
59	LIFE
58	Economist
55	Rolling Stone
54	*Business Week
54	*Psychology Today
53	Consumer Reports
53	Ebony
52	History Today
50	Macleans
50	Natural History
50	Popular Mechanics
50	Smithsonian
49	Omni
48	*Reader's Digest
47	*Good Housekeeping
46	Harper's Magazine
44	*American Heritage
44	New Scientist
44	New Yorker
43	New Republic
42	Health
41	Booklist
40	Parents
40	Teen
39	Jet
39	National Wildlife
38	Better Homes & Gardens
38	Ladies' Home Journal
37	Current History
37	World Press Review
36	Car & Driver
36	Foreign Affairs
36	Saturday Evening Post
36	School Library Journal
36	*Science
35	Environment
35	*National Review
34	Motor Trend
34	UNESCO Courier
33	Vogue
32	Atlantic Monthly
32	Hot Rod
32	Outdoor Life
31	Glamour
31	Money
31	Phi Delta Kappan
31	Vital Speeches of the Day
30	Americas
30	Astronomy
30	Women's Sport & Fitness
29	Education Digest
29	McCalls
29	National Geographic World
29	People Weekly
29	Popular Photography
29	Road & Track
28	Congressional Digest
28	Kiplinger's Personal
28	Finance Magazine
28	Mademoiselle
28	Prevention
28	Scholastic Update
27	Audubon
27	Field & Stream
27	MacWorld
27	USA Today
25	Commonweal
25	Fortune
25	*People
24	Art News
24	Atlantic
24	Byte
24	Christian Century
24	International Wildlife
24	Macuser
24	UN Chronicle (Quarterly)
23	English Journal
23	Futurist
23	Media and Methods
23	New Internationalist
22	America
22	American History Illustrated
22	Essence
22	Forbes
22	Runner's World
22	Sport
21	Geographical Magazine
21	Ms
21	New York Times Magazine
21	PC Computing

Appendix E

Multiculturalism and Multilingualism

Richard Barter

Central to the mission of effective international school libraries

Providing effective libraries and library services in International Schools is made both more difficult and more rewarding by the centrality of pluralism in our students, staff, and curricula. More and more one finds, in our broader International School community, recognition that we have not done enough to emphasise these important features of our library collections and services, and that we still have a long way to go before they are universally enshrined as an inescapable part of every International School – and every International School library. As with many other areas of professional practice, literature and theory specific to International Schools is sparse. However, there are some wonderful materials produced in English-speaking countries that are clearly relevant, and which can be 'adapted' to serve our needs.

The purpose of this Appendix to *Effective Libraries* is not to offer a detailed study of the major schools of thought, or a long, annotated bibliography. Rather, it is intended to be a brief précis, a condensed summary, of current schools of thought, and will hopefully highlight perhaps not the best, most profound literature on the subject, but rather fairly easy to locate, not particularly 'heavy' sources of further reading or study– as well as practical examples of effective practices from International Schools around the world.

Multilingualism

Far too often one hears from schools that they would like to do more to support multilingualism among their students, but that their primary mission is to teach English and, in an era of tight budgets and limited financial and human resources, multilingual support and materials are simply 'extras' that the school cannot afford. This distressing school of thought ignores what we have learned, and what research has increasingly proven, about how children learn language and languages. Simply put, to maximise a child's development and achievement, it is necessary to support and encourage continued growth in all of the languages of the child's world. This has enormous implications for schools in terms of ESL and other language programme options — and there is increasingly a call for all International Schools to formulate and write down some sort of 'School Language Policy' document that will guide further work in this area.

For many students in International Schools, there are at least three languages active in the child's world: English (assuming that that is the language of instruction of the school), the host country language (as most schools — and many host countries — require students to learn this language), and what is often called the student's Mother Tongue. It is worth noting that Mother Tongue does not necessarily mean the language of the child's mother(!) — I have also heard it referred to as First Language, Preferred Language, Home Language, and much of the more serious literature in the field resorts to using shorthand notation, calling it L1. The great advantage of using the term Mother Tongue is that in many, many languages (and in virtually all European languages) the equivalent term is a direct translation (Langue Maternelle, Muttersprache, *etc*) and calling it Mother Tongue simply makes communication with parents and others easier. Indeed, a child may have several Mother Tongues, if he or she comes from a bi- or tri-lingual family, for example. According to *The Cambridge Encyclopedia of Language*, parenthetically, less than a quarter of the world's nations give official recognition to two languages, and only six recognise three or more — although there are 4000-5000 (or 2000-3000, depending on the source) languages on Earth, in less than 200 countries! Obviously, then, the vast majority of people on the planet — and in our pluralist International Schools — are multilingual.

While school administrators and librarians will want to seek professional guidance and support from their trained ESL staff, the research is very clear that the stronger the student's Mother Tongue skills, the better their English language skills will be, as they will already have a strong language 'base' to build upon. Very few schools will be able to offer formal language instruction in the whole range of Mother Tongues represented in their student body. For most schools, support for Mother Tongue development will consist of workshops and other outreach efforts to educate parents about the vital role they play in helping their child continue to develop strong literacy skills in his or her Mother Tongue. It may be possible for the school to act as a 'facilitator,' helping groups of parents with a common language locate a tutor, or offer use of school facilities. School librarians, simply put, must be equal partners in curriculum planning and in the academic life of the school and, because good school libraries put 'service' as their first priority, the library is a logical place to make available to parents literature about these issues.

The most vital role that the library can play, however, is by providing access to a selection of books and other materials in many languages — giving children and parents the opportunity to borrow materials in their language(s). Having such a collection also, not insignificantly, makes a strong statement about the value that the school places on the richness of linguistic diversity. The problems of building up such a collection can be huge, but they are not insurmountable. The rewards are enormous. I have seen a child freshly arrived from Finland literally screaming at being plopped down in a country and a school where no one spoke her language nor she theirs. The key to calming her down, and to allowing the teacher to build a bond of trust and understanding with her, was a book featuring the ubiquitous little dog Spot, in Finnish, speedily fetched from the school's library. Similarly I remember a bright boy from China who was very resistant to speaking English with the other children until he discovered how impressed they were that he could explain to them what the strange Chinese pictographs meant in a book about dragons that the class was looking at. Much of the 'evidence' of this sort is anecdotal, and librarians in International Schools can benefit greatly from sharing such stories with one another.

So, where can you locate these 'foreign language' books? There is, alas, no universal source, and a bit of ingenuity is called for. The best bit of advice is to start small, and to think locally. Parent volunteers, who are familiar with your library and the types of books that the children use and enjoy, are a great resource. Ask them to buy a small number of books when next they are on home leave, for which you will reimburse them. Very often, it has been my experience, they will get so enthusiastic about the project that they will spend much more than the, say, US$100 that you authorised, and will simply present purchases over that amount as a gift – and more often than not gifts from parents will be a major source of growth in your collection, either materials that they purchased specifically for the school, or from families who are moving on and donate books they no longer want.

Similarly, contact local embassies or consulates and see if they offer some sort of support. Some will authorise funds, and I know of one European country whose national library service will send a large carton of materials as 'inter-library loan' if there is a formally organised Mother Tongue class. While it can be difficult to find bookshops or publishers in a specific country that can or will export, it is not impossible, and a good way to locate sources of materials is to contact an International School in that country. I have known librarians in different countries to set up an exchange, agreeing to buy and ship one another an agreed amount worth of books in their respective host country languages.

Supportive members of your own teaching staff or administration are another source – find out who's going where on holiday, and ask them to do a little shopping for you while they're away. A final useful tip is to think about where you usually buy books and audiovisual software for your library - and what minority populations there are in that country.

There are several good sources of books and tapes in various Indian languages, as well as things like Greek or Turkish, in the United Kingdom. Many mainstream book suppliers in the United States can provide materials in Spanish, and there are several good outlets for East Asian languages in Canada. Another interesting approach is to consider magazines. Most international jobbers or subscription agencies (like EBSCO, for example) can provide almost anything. Because of political and economic change, for many years the popular Russian magazine for children *Misha* was the only Russian-language resource readily available. I know of a school in Spain where the arrival of each month's new issue of the Korean-language version of the *Readers' Digest* is an eagerly awaited event! Some languages are harder to locate than others, so a good rule of thumb is to get what you can get, when and where you can get it. Very often, as well, the physical quality of the paper or bindings might not be as high as you would expect to find in an English-language book. Learn to accept this – and learn a few good, basic book repair and rebinding techniques!

Finally, a quick word about culture, as it relates to language. There is a delicate balancing act involved in finding the right balance between books written in a language and books that will be popular because they are translations of works that the students might know, for example, from English. Booklist publishes occasional annotated bibliographies of popular books in specific languages, and many smaller nations, I have found, have Institutes or other organisations dedicated to promoting children's literature in that country that can provide useful information. I remember a specific example (and, although I will make the school and the librarian anonymous, I hope they will forgive me using them as an example) of a very good school, with excellent libraries, in Germany. The librarian confided in me that she knew and understood all of this theory about the need to support literacy development in as many of the languages of her students as possible, but was finding that German books simply weren't being read – either by Mother Tongue speakers or by students taking German as a foreign language. I asked her to describe her collection to me. Of course, it consisted of all of the German 'classics' and, when I pushed her, she admitted that no one read Goethe or Schiller in English either! I sent her to a local bookshop known to have an excellent children's section and told her to buy anything that she recognised as being popular in English. Once the Beverly Cleary and Judy Blume and Roald Dahl (in translation) started flying off her shelves, she became more confident, and her collection grew to include Christina Nöstlinger, Erwin Moser, Ursula Fuchs, Tomas Brezina and many other German-language authors who were equally, if not more, popular with her students!

Some suggestions for further reading

Crystal, David (1987). *The Cambridge Encyclopedia of Language.* Cambridge: Cambridge University Press.
This is a hefty reference book that is well worth having to support student project work as well as for it's useful summaries of the major issues relating to language and language acquisition. There may be a more recent edition, or a less-expensive paperback, available.

Cummins, Jim.
Jim Cummins, an Irishman now working in Canada, is one of the genuine giants of the English as a Second Language field. Any books or articles by him will be relevant, well-supported by research, and up-to-date.

Fitzgerald, Jill. (1993) Literacy and students who are learning English as a second language. *The Reading Teacher,* 46 (8).
Her point, based on review of the research, is that what works in one language will work in another! This will be especially useful if, for example, your English curriculum is 'Whole Language' based. You may be able to locate a copy of this journal in your school, as many schools receive it as part of their membership in the International Reading Association.

Harding, Edith, and Riley, Philip (1986). *The Bilingual Family: A Handbook for Parents.* Cambridge: Cambridge University Press.
A wonderful short book that explains complicated issues in an easy-to-understand way - not only to parents, but also to confused (or curious) librarians (or teachers and administrators!).

Katzner, Kenneth (1986). *The Languages of the World.* (rev.ed). London: Routledge & Kegan Paul.
If you can't find this specific book, look for something similar. A necessary and vital reference tool for learning the difference between Czech and Slovak (not huge) or Bahasa Malaysia and Malayalam (very huge! One is spoken in Malaysia, the other in India - the closeness of the names is just a coincidence).

Smith, Frank (1985). *Reading without Nonsense.* (2nd ed). New York: Teachers College Press.
While not specifically 'multilingual' in focus, Frank Smith can explain, even for the layperson, the process of learning to read better than almost anyone else. While this is perhaps his most seminal work, also keep an eye out for: Joining the Literacy Club: Further Essays into Education (London: Heinemann, 1988) which concludes with a wonderful essay about being reminded how to teach reading by trying, as an adult, to read a picture book in long-ago-studied Greek, with a seven-year-old girl as his teacher. Inspirational.

One final suggestion: The International Reading Association (800 Barksdale Road, PO Box 8139, Newark Delaware, 19714-8139, USA) and the National Association for the Education of Young Children (1509 16th Street NW, Washington DC, 20036-1846, USA) produce a wide range of excellent resources. Particularly noteworthy are low-cost brochures and pamphlets intended for distribution to parents and others. Many of these titles are available in Spanish translations, with a very limited number available in French. Similarly, a fair number of the 'Digests' produced by the various ERIC Clearinghouses can also be obtained in Spanish, and plans have been announced to offer translations into other languages as well.

Multiculturalism

One of the most satisfactory trends that I have noticed in almost a decade of offering workshops and publishing articles about multiculturalism in International Schools is the now near-universal acceptance of multiculturalism as a fundamental principal of international education. This was not always so, and it is a welcome change. There is, however, an inherent danger whenever a particular instructional theory or educational philosophy becomes some sort of ubiquitous 'brand name.' While there are certainly a huge number of excellent schools doing excellent work, there are also those where 'Whole Language' or 'Constructivism' (or 'Multiculturalism'!) are mere words, the theory and practice little in evidence in the school's instructional programme. School librarians have a special opportunity and responsibility to play a major role in professional development activities within the school, by making available a wide range of quality professional reading, and also the sorts of resources needed to effectively support the school's stated educational philosophy.

Even a quick glance at the professional literature, or at catalogues of school books and educational materials, reveals that the word 'multicultural' has become a generic catchall. The first step, then, in achieving a 'multicultural' school and school library is to figure out exactly what one means by the term! A particularly good place to start, and it is something that a great many schools might actually have stuffed in the back of a cupboard somewhere, is a themed issue of the important professional journal *Language Arts* that was published in March 1993. In a variety of articles different authors look at the question of multiculturalism and multicultural children's books from several different angles. Much more obscure, but to my way of thinking a seminal work, is a fascinating article called *Multiculturalism: E Pluribus Plures* by the well-known American educationalist Diane Ravitch. Published in *The American Scholar* (Summer 1990) this piece is well-worth the trouble it might take to locate a copy - and librarians are reminded that ECIS maintains an excellent Information Service that may be able to be of assistance in locating this and other journal articles. I've not tested this hypothesis, but I suspect it might also be possible to locate a copy using the American educational resource clearinghouse called ERIC.

Ravitch gives a good introduction to the history of multiculturalism (in the United States), and posits that the movement has actually split into two very distinct branches, one of which she finds admirable, the other particularly dangerous and harmful. The admirable branch is what she calls 'pluralist multiculturalism' and is a philosophy that accepts and welcomes that culture, in our societies and in our schools, is in constant flux, constantly absorbing new influences and ideas.

The other more dangerous branch of multiculturalism, the one that leaves the movement open to charges that it breeds intolerance and 'reverse racism' is what Ravitch calls 'particularist multiculturalism.' A particularist viewpoint is one that views people as groups, not as individuals. It views culture as something that is set in stone. This is a particularly inappropriate model for International Schools where it is clear that a great many of our students are 'third culture' kids – that the experience of living and studying in different cultures has dramatically altered the students' cultural outlook. To use a concrete example, based on a student I worked with several years ago: A 'Korean' who had never lived in Korea, was now living is Spain, but had spent many happy years in Canada and whose Mother Tongue was, for all intents and purposes, English. To the particularlists, this boy was and always will be 'Korean' (and, by the way, there are well-meaning books and articles that will tell you what kinds of learning styles and behavioural patterns to expect from a 'Korean.' So much for child-centred education!) To a pluralist, however, he is an individual, with his own individual cultural and linguistic background and roots. To see how easy it is to fall unknowingly into the 'particularist' trap, flip through one of the published directories of International Schools and see how many schools actually take pride in listing the number of different national groups represented in their student population. Not only does this ignore the 'third culture' reality of many of these students' lives, it fails to see the glorious and unique culture that is created within each and every school by the intermixing and intermingling of so many culturally diverse individuals. By celebrating the diversity of the groups, they miss the diversity of the individuals. I am perhaps overstating here, but I think it is an important point to make.

How does one go about building up a library collection of multicultural books for children and young adults? The terse answer is to say that one doesn't. Multiculturalism (of the pluralist stripe) is not a curriculum add-on, not something that gets hauled out of mothballs once a year on UN Day. It is, rather, a way of thinking, a way of learning, a way of seeing the world – and it is integrated into every resource decision that we make. The American review journals Booklist and School Library Journal, which are vital selection tools, do a very good job of drawing attention to books that do a particularly good job of revealing other cultures, and identifying books that do a particularly bad job of it. I often joke that the ultimate particularist children's book would be a nightmare tome called *Jamilla and Her Mother go to the Market and Take a Stand against Society's Oppression of Women of Color by Buying only Non-exploitive Produce*. While this is a joke, there are a frightful number of books like this which are not jokes, but which are deeply misguided attempts to produce 'instructional' literature for children. Harriet Rohmer, the founder of the non-profit (pluralist multicultural) publisher Children's Book Press once defined multicultural literature, in the issue of Language Arts that I mention above, as 'a literature of inclusion: stories from and stories about all our children.'

It would be a shame for a wonderful book like Ed Young's Caldecott Award winning book *Lon Po Po*, a Little Red Riding Hood story with a

Chinese setting, to be used only as a 'Chinese' book. It's good because it's a wonderfully well-written and well-illustrated story, not because it's 'multicultural.' Similarly, it would be a shame if Eric Kimmel's delightful *Herschel and the Hannukah Goblins* were only to be used or shared with children when the annual 'Hannukah Unit' rolled around, or his *Anansi and the Moss-Covered Rock* only gets looked at when 'African' tales are called for. Examples of truly wonderful literature for children and young adults that gets branded as 'multicultural,' overlooking the fact that the books are amazing examples of their art, abound.

A common complaint that I hear from teachers and librarians about multicultural books is that 'the students just don't want to read them.' Almost without exception it has been my experience that children don't want to read bad, boring books (see the note about Margaret Meek in the selected readings listed below). *Jamilla and her Mother Go to the Market...* etc and books like it, are boring, stilted, and badly written. *Lon Po Po* isn't. It's that simple. If the multicultural materials in your school or in your library are boring, particularist-flavoured works, no one will want to read them. As with the story that I told earlier about books in German, if you fill your shelves and classrooms with good, enjoyable, well-written and well-produced books, they will get read, whether they are multicultural or not. And if your book collection contains works that will allow a child to absorb cultural detail through the plot, dialogue, or illustrations, then you will have taken a huge step forward in terms of helping to establish the kinds of conditions where pluralist multiculturalism can blossom and grow.

One final word of warning about a problem that is perhaps especially relevant to International Schools. Very often books are published simultaneously on both sides of the Atlantic, or an American publisher will later bring out an edition of a book that has sold particularly well in the UK (or vice versa). It is not unusual for editors to make slight changes to grammar, spelling, punctuation, and the like, to reflect current usage in the country where the edition is published. Much less often, but much more of a problem, is when names, places, events, and the like are altered. For years I had a British edition of a popular Dr Seuss title, wherein the publisher had replaced the word Dollars with Pounds. Not a huge issue, not bad enough to make me replace the book, but it did mean that the rhyme and rhythm didn't scan, something that seemed so un-Seuss-ian. Recently, however, I was reading a British edition of the popular (American) young adult novel *The Wave*. There were, from what I could see, minor changes in punctuation and vocabulary. Nothing too radical. Then I got to a scene where a bunch of American students were sitting around an American locker room discussing their weight, which is an issue in playing American football - but they were doing so in stones! I ordered a replacement copy from the US the next day. Portrayals of any cultural group should be accurate, and any cultural details contained in the story, dialogue, or illustrations should be equally accurate. Replacing US style weights and measures with metric counterparts in a science or cookbook published in Britain is wholly understandable. In fiction, however, it distorts the representation of the culture that is supposedly being portrayed. It would be a lot easier to read an English translation of Tolstoy if one didn't have to grapple with all of the Russian patronymics – but it also wouldn't be Russian. It wouldn't be Tolstoy.

Some suggestions for further reading:

Madigan, D (1993) The politics of multicultural literature for children and adolescents: combining perspectives and conversations. *Language Arts,* 70.
An article from this special 'multicultural' issue of LA. Especially interesting in light of Ravitch's particularist/pluralist argument. The pluralist Harriet Rohmer quote from above is from here, and is contrasted nicely with some amazingly particularist claptrap.

McElmeel, SL (1993) 'Toward a real multiculturalism,' *School Library Journal.* 39 (11).
Not an outstanding article, but a good overview of the issues - and a magazine that is widely subscribed to by International School librarians.

Meek, Margaret (1988). *How Texts Teach What Readers Learn.* Stroud: Thimble Press.
I am including this wonderful little booklet (it's only 48 pages long) because it deserves to be much better known outside of the United Kingdom. There's nothing 'multicultural' about it – just the clearest, most succinct statement I have ever read about what makes a good children's book.

Ravitch, Diane (1990). Multiculturalism: E Pluribus Plures. *The American Scholar,* Summer.
As mentioned in the text above, I'm breaking my own rule by suggesting something that is rather heavy-going scholarship, and hard to find. It is, however, well worth the effort. Outstanding.

Wurzel, Jaime (ed) (1988). *Toward Multiculturalism: A Reader in Multicultural Education.* Yarmouth, ME: Intercultural Press.
In addition to interesting chapters and essays, the introduction by Wurzel (who frequently leads workshops and summer seminars) is a good, concise outline of multicultural education, including an easily understood and adaptable seven-step process.

Yokota, June (1993). Issues in selecting multicultural children's literature. *Language Arts,* 70.
Another article from this special themed issue. Her one sentence definition of what is a multicultural children's book is the best I've ever read.

Finally, and a bit boldly, I will suggest that if you would like to read longer, more detailed discussion about the points raised in this Appendix, you might want to track down some of my (!) published articles, which formed much of the basis for this simplified version. The three I would recommend are:

Barter, R (1996). Global Village, Global Values, Skepsis, *The International Schools Association Magazine,* 4, ppXVI-XIX.

Barter, R (1996). Multiculturalism and libraries: and still the battle rages. *New Library World,* 97 (1128), p10-14.

Barter, R (1994). Multiculturalism and multilingualism: what it means in practice. *International Schools Journal,* 27, p31-40.

Richard Barter Jr, Head Librarian, International College, Beirut , and Co-ordinator for International Schools, International Association of School Librarianship.

Appendix F

Staff, Programme and Services Assessment Schemes

Two schemes are suggested as examples of programme assessments, and a single sample is provided for staff performance evaluation as well as the pro-forma used in the ECIS accreditation process.

The last two items can be viewed and downloaded from the ECIS web site <www.ecis.org/libraries>

1. **Staff performance model**

    A model that has been updated from the first edition of this publication

2. **ECIS Accreditation standard and effective practices for the library media centre**

    Developed by the European Council of International Schools' Committee on Accreditation.

3. **School library media programme profile and alignment document**
    This was developed by the New England Educational Media Association to work with accreditation process for the New England Association of Schools and Colleges, where assessment focuses on teaching and learning.

4. **Pitts-Stripling model**
    This is a more performance-based scheme that assesses a level of performance on a scale from deficient to exemplary, and provides recognisable benchmarks for each indicator.

Staff Performance Model sample

Observable performance standards and activities are:
1. Demonstrating knowledge of content and curriculum
    a Co-ordination with classroom teachers
    b Promotion of discriminating reading, listening, and viewing skills

2. Provides appropriate learning experiences for students
    a Evidence of a variety of teaching strategies and techniques
    b Accommodation of learning styles
    c Objectives appropriate to development level of students

3. Demonstrates appropriate planning
    a Established current status as a beginning for growth
    b Has a 3-5 year plan strategic plan for the programme
    c Resources are organised, well-selected, inventories accurate, records available

4. Manages instruction and student behaviour
    a Develops active lesson plans, communicates expectations, keeps students on task, uses time effectively, maintains discipline
    b Welcomes and works with all students to the centre
    c Maintains a welcoming environment
    d Disciplines effectively

5. Demonstrates strong interpersonal and communication skills
    a Demonstrates respect for all students
    b Builds personal relationships with faculty and students
    c Provides multi-cultural materials and builds respect for diversity

6. Demonstrates Library Management Skills
    a Develops policies and procedures to facilitate student and teacher use
    b Develops the budget out of the long-range plan.
    c Demonstrates fiscal responsibility
    d Organises the collection and maintains appropriate indexes and automation systems

7. Provides library media services
    a Maintains and develops new services for the teaching and learning community
    b Makes use of community liaisons and resources
    c Regularly scans needs of users to develop and extend the programme of services

8. Interpersonal Relationships and Personal Growth
    a Consistently demonstrates ability to work collegially with all users.
    b Participates fully in school activities
    c Self-evaluates
    d Encourages intellectual curiosity and continual learning for self and others

Accreditation

The accreditation process provides the school and its library an opportunity to articulate and assess its roles within the educational community. The self-study process empowers a group of colleagues to examine the library programme, its services, purpose, organization, and management through a collegial lens and identify its strengths and weaknesses as it strives to achieve its mission, goals, and contribution to the overall instructional programme of the school. It provides a rare opportunity to take the time to look inward to see how well perceptions meet realities and provides a prioritised plan to resolve deficiencies.

The following section details the ECIS Standards for Accreditation and Effective Practices for the Library/Media Centre (LMC). During the period of self-study the committee established to evaluate the LMC reviews current practice with reference to the school's philosophy and objectives and the standards for accreditation.

Library/Media centre

Introduction

Library/media centre programmes in overseas/international schools take on various forms from traditional libraries to classroom libraries to technologically advanced media centres. Whatever form the school's library/media programme takes, it should be an integral component of the school and it should act as an extension of individual classrooms and/or programmes.

Many of the basic skills learned in other programme areas may be learned or reinforced by the library/media programme; other skills will be learned firsthand during library instruction. Still other knowledge will be gained and minds broadened by a student's experience with library resources themselves.

International school library/media centres optimally should include three categories of facilities:
- Learning facilities – in which the students, individually or as a group, are brought together with media for the purpose of learning
- Facilities for storage and access – in which media in various forms are catalogued, stored and made accessible for learning situations
- Production and supporting facilities – in which media in a variety of forms are produced to meet particular learning requirements and where teaching staff and students receive assistance and support in the effective and efficient use of media and technology

Standards for Accreditation

1. There shall be a library and/or media centre of adequate size and resources to meet the educational needs of the students
2. Materials shall be maintained in a manner, which makes them accessible to students, and staff. The library collection shall be catalogued
3. The library collection shall be adequate to provide for non-school connected reading for relaxation
4. There shall be adequate orientation and instruction of students in the use of media equipment and of the library's reference materials
5. The library/media centre staff, both professional and non-professional, shall be adequate to provide effective service to the students and faculty
6. There shall be a library selection policy and one for challenged materials
7. There shall be in-service opportunities available to new staff members focusing on the extent of library holding and media equipment

Effective practices

As a development from, or practical expression of, the basic Standards for Accreditation referred to above, the following practices are commonly found in schools of quality. The school should consider each practice and check whether its own effectiveness is Very Effective; Effective; Reasonably Effective; Ineffective; and Not Applicable.

Policy

1. There is a library policy agreed by all staff. It includes a selection policy and policy for challenged materials.
2. The board has policies relating to library acquisitions, censorship and development
3. The librarian is involved in curriculum development and is aware of what students are being taught
4. Materials and equipment for the library/media centre are selected on the basis of their contribution to the overall school programme
5. Teachers and students are given orientation in the use of materials and equipment in the library/media centre
6. The library/media centre staff promotes the effective utilisation of library/media resources by students and staff
7. There are planned means of evaluating the library's effectiveness *eg* number of users, analysis of age and frequency of use of stock

Accommodation

8. The library/media centre is centrally located, easily accessible and open at such times as will encourage optimum use of the materials and equipment

9 The library/media centre is comfortable, well-lit, attractive, inviting, clearly sign-posted and easy to use
10 The library/media centre is sufficiently spacious to enable browsing, borrowing, relaxed reading and reference and has adequate facilities for private group and class study

Staffing

11 The library/media centre staff, both professional and non-professional, is adequate to provide effective service to the students and staff
12 The professional members of the library/media staff have specialised preparation in the organization and administration of library/media centre services, maintain awareness of current thinking and are an integral part of the regular staff

Funding

13 Financial provision is made for the maintenance and continuous development of the library/media centre and services.

Collection

14 The collection of books, periodicals, reference materials and equipment, including Information Technology, is adequate in quantity and quality to meet the stated goals of the educational programme and the special needs of a school in an international setting with a student body of an international character.
15 A portion of the library collection is devoted to professional education books and periodicals, provided for the professional reading and growth of the teaching staff
16 Audio-visual equipment is readily available to teachers and is maintained in working condition.

Appendix G

Library Programme

John Royce

Research Links and Student Achievement

Effective libraries, effective learning - notes from the research on the impact of library programmes on learning

Time and again, research studies show that quality library services make positive contributions to students' academic and social achievement. Effective libraries affect performance. Despite this, many schools fail to provide sufficient resources and staffing which enable those quality services to achieve the desired results in the instructional programme. In this appendix, we look at some of the reasons why some school libraries fall dreadfully short of their potential resulting in the educational community's overall failure to benefit, as it should.

It will be interesting to watch for improvement in examination results in those schools which are permitted to take part in the IB Middle and Primary Years Programmes. To be admitted, schools must have a learning ethos, for these are learning-centred curricula: the aim is to make children independent, lifelong learners ... which are precisely the aims of today's library programmes.

McDonald (1988, pxiv) is one who points to the catch-22 situation: school library media specialists often say that they would become more involved in curriculum and design of instruction if they had time or if there was someone to take over the clerical tasks. No time leads to no evidence of involvement with the instructional programme and no evidence for additional staff or a flexible schedule. These media specialists must accept the fact that only a demonstration of benefits is likely to convince administrators and teachers that the instructional programme could be improved.

Boardman (1991, p16) concurs: Until some respected body of research says 'here's proof,' few schools are going to put libraries on their priority list. Pender (1987, p98) concurs: Only when high-quality school library service is clearly linked to effective learning will the teaching profession as a whole become firmly committed to the role of the resource centre in the school.

These arguments fail, because the proof does exist.

In *What Works*, Haycock (1992) summarises nearly 600 doctoral theses and dissertations on school librarianship. Many of these deal directly or indirectly with issues of impact, and the vast majority of these show that libraries and librarians really do make a positive difference in the educational process.

Didier (1988) also offers a review of studies whose main focus is impact; she too finds that most studies reveal positive impact.

Some of these studies are single school case studies, and some are studies at district, state or national levels. Particularly telling are those which provide without-and-with or before-and-after comparisons, since these are more able to limit the influence of other or outside factors.

The studies reviewed by Didier and Haycock tend to be North American in origin, but there is much research in other countries.

In Australia, Todd (1994) found that all students in his information literacy group made significant and lasting gains over the traditionally-taught group. He found students of different abilities benefited in different ways, but that all benefited.

In Britain, Hughes (1993) similarly carried out a study to demonstrate the effects of flexible learning as compared with traditional classes in his school; all students in flexible learning group benefited, pupils of high ability gaining most; significantly, the effects persisted over time.

Mortimer and Mortimer (1994) investigated the before-and-after effects of appointing associate staff to schools; they suggest methods of analysing benefits and disbenefits and of assessing cost-effectiveness of the appointments. They show the effects on attitudes towards lessons, on learning and in research skills in those schools in which library appointments were made. They show how teaching was felt to be a happier, more rewarding experience in those particular schools.

Lealand's report on the New Zealand experiment (1990) showed that even though many teacher-librarians felt that they had not made the impact they had hoped to make, they were misunderstood and teachers' and administrators' perceptions of their roles did not always coincide with their own perceptions; real impact was made. Lealand concluded:

> Despite continuing problems and an uncertain future, the introduction of trained teacher-librarians into New Zealand schools has been successful. It has encouraged a wider and more diverse use of resources, introduced different perspectives on teaching and learning and perhaps, most importantly, promoted self-esteem amongst considerable numbers of students, who are now realising that the acquisition of knowledge through resource-based learning can be both a pleasurable and a powerful process. (Lealand, p90.)

Perhaps the most telling of recent studies into the impact of the library programme is that of Lance (1993). Using published statistics of over 200 Colorado schools, demonstrated to be representative of schools throughout the state and nation, Lance isolated the many factors which have been suggested as contributing to academic achievement, such as family size and educational background, family income, class size, teacher-pupil ratio, teacher qualifications and experience and so on. Isolating them singly and in combination, he concluded:

> Among school and community predictors of academic achievement, the size of the LMC staff and collection is second only to the absence of at-risk conditions, particularly poverty and low educational attainment among adults (Lance, p92).

As for the factors, which a school might control, he concluded:

> The size of a library media centre's staff and collection is the best school predictor of academic achievement (Lance, p92).

At about the same time as Lance's study was published, Krashen (1993) published a survey of over 200 research studies in reading; these would confirm that free voluntary reading enables learning in general. Loertscher, commenting on the importance of both of these studies, suggested:

> Not only are the two studies a powerful argument for the support of strong library media programs as an essential component in every school, but they put the burden of proof back on those who claim the contrary. It is doubtful that any evidence can be mounted to show that good library media programs don't make a difference (Lance, p144).

The research evidence is there, but it is not enough. Even in New Zealand, where the three-year experiment was so successful and so widely applauded by those who benefited, the ending of State funding led to closure of many library programs. Libraries continue to be under-utilised and librarians bypassed, even while calls are made for better use of resources, for more individualised learning, for the skills of information literacy to be inculcated. It is not a lack of research evidence, which prevents many libraries playing the role demanded by the literature.

The reasons must be sought elsewhere. The taxonomy-based models described in the Appendix may provide some of the answers. So much depends on the school ethos: a learning school invests in its library. This means investment in stock but it also means investment in staff. Loertscher and Ho and Bowie's multi-system study (1988) has shown that school libraries do not begin, cannot begin, to yield dividends until the school librarian has full-time clerical support. There seems to be a threshold at which the library media programme begins to pay the kind of dividends expected from the investment made in it. This threshold is a staff consisting of a full-time professional and a full-time clerical person. This finding was not only statistically significant but was the single most important variable in an excellent library media programme.

A library media centre has such a heavy warehousing function that a professional without full-time clerical assistance gets bogged down in the clerical burdens of the centre. (Loertscher, Ho, and Bowie, p.78.) And beyond investment in stock and staff is the school itself. There needs also to be a learning-centred approach to education. The view prevalent in the 1980s notwithstanding, the librarian alone cannot change anything. Brown (1988) stated: It is an impossible task, based on a naive notion of change, for the teacher-librarian within a particular school to attempt to single-handedly change teaching practice in the school... The literature on change in education reveals that change will only occur if administrators and teachers feel a definite need for it and if there is a broad base of support.

The support of the school's administration team is vital. The support of the school's teaching faculty is vital. Again there is research evidence to support the view that it is a total team effort.

Corr (1981), Pickard (1990) and Heeks and Kinnell (1994) are amongst many whose research results show that the role of the principal is one of the most important factors in the development of an effective school library programme. And in their study, Streatfield and Markless (1994) found that:

> The single most important factor leading to effective use of libraries in both primary and secondary schools was a positive attitude by teachers. Teachers are in a position to prevent library use during lesson time and to discourage interest in the library; they can also provide a range of opportunities for children to use the library, work with the library staff in planning and delivering library-based topics, help children develop the information handling skills required to make effective use of the library resources, and encourage children to make active use of books, non-book materials and the school library (as well as local public libraries). (Streatfield and Markless p.179)

It will be interesting to watch for improvement in examination results in those schools which are permitted to take part in the IB Middle Years Programme. To be admitted, schools must have a learning ethos, for this is a learning-centred curriculum: the aim is to make children independent learners and lifelong learners. These are also the aims of those schools providing library services at the highest level.

And yet, and yet... Research evidence alone does not change attitudes. Those unwilling or unable to make the change, have unfortunately no need to take up Loertscher's challenge and provide evidence to disprove the impact of a strong library programme. They need only do nothing. And therein lies the challenge.

Bibliography

Boardman, Edna M (1991). Are you keeping the books straight? Our enduring image problem and how we can reshape it. *The Book Report*, May-June, pp14-16.

Brown, Jean (1988). Changing teaching practice to meet current expectations: implications for teacher-librarians. *Emergency Librarian*, 16, Nov-Dec, pp13-14.

Corr, Graham P (1981) Where do we go from here?: The teacher-librarian's involvement in curriculum planning and implementation. *Australian School Librarian*, 18 (1), pp5-13.

Didier, Elaine K. (1988) Research on the impact of school library media programs on student achievement: implications for school library media professionals. In: McDonald, FB (comp). *The Emerging School Library Media Program Readings.* pp25-44. Englewood, CO: Libraries Unlimited

Haycock, Ken. (1992) *What Works*: Research about Teaching and Learning through the School's Library Resource Center. Seattle, WA: Rockwell Press.

Heeks, Peggy & Kinnell, Margaret (1994). *School Libraries at Work (Library and Information Research Report)*. Wetherby: The British Library Board.

Hughes, Mike (1993). *Flexible Learning: Evidence Examined. Teaching and Learning. series.* Stafford: Network Educational Press.

Krashen, Stephen (1993). *The Power of Reading: Insights from the Research.* Englewood, CO: Libraries Unlimited.

Lance, Keith Curry, Welborn, Lynda & Hamilton-Pennell, Christine (1993). *The Impact of School Library Media Centers on Academic Achievement.* Castle Rock, CO: Hi Willow Research and Publishing.

Lealand, Geoff (1990). *The Educational Impact of the Appointment of Full-time Trained Teacher-Librarians: Final Report.* Wellington: New Zealand Council for Educational Research.

Loertscher, David V (1993) Presenting the Colorado Study. In Lance, KC et al, *The Impact of School Library Media Centers on Academic Achievement.* pp144. Castle Rock, CO: Hi Willow Research and Publishing.

Loertscher, David V, Ho, May Lein & Bowie, Melvin M (1988). 'Exemplary elementary schools' and their library media centers: a research report. In McDonald, Frances Beck, (comp) *The Emerging School Library Media Program: Readings.* pp68-82. Englewood, CO: Libraries Unlimited

McDonald, Frances Beck (comp) (1988). *The Emerging School Library Media Program: Readings.* Englewood, CO: Libraries Unlimited, Inc.

Mortimore, Peter & Mortimore, Jo with Thomas, Hywel (1994). *Managing Associate Staff: Innovation in Primary and Secondary Schools.* London: Paul Chapman Publishing.

Pender, Kevin (1987). Some aspects of school library development in England and Wales: an English school librarian's point of view. *School Library Media Quarterly*, 15 (2), pp96-98.

Pickard, Patricia White (1990). The Instructional Consultant Role of the School Library Media Specialist: A Research Study. (Dissertation, Georgia State University, Atlanta GA,). ERIC, ED 328 276.

Streatfield, David & Markless, Sharon (1994). Invisible learning? *The contribution of school libraries to teaching and learning.* Report to the British Library Research and Development Department on the 'Effective School Library' Research Project. Library and Information Research Report, 98. Boston Spa: British Library Research and Development Department,

Todd, Ross J (1994). Information literacy and learning: IASL report of Australian research. *IASL Newsletter* 23, April, p5-6.

John Royce, Librarian, International School of Hamburg, Germany, 1998

Research Summary, Taxonomy of Library Programmes

Several models of library programmes have been developed, typically demonstrating three or four levels of service, phases of development or level of involvement with the school curriculum. The models include criteria or indicators by which one's own services can be matched and measured.

By their very choice of terms, the models imply that low-level services are inferior to high-level services; they may also suggest that progress to the highest levels may be achieved either by evolution or by revolution. As a school moves up the 'ladder,' the monetary investment in the library facility, collection of resources, equipment, and staffing begins to pay dividends. At low levels, they are expensive; at high levels they strongly influence student achievement.

Nevertheless, most authorities do state that the library may operate at various levels of service during the day and through the year, and that the needs of subject departments may differ and thus require different levels of service at various times throughout the year.

Services are offered on the basis of the school programme and the availability of personnel, resources and facilities. Priorities are determined by the individual schools since not all services will be offered in every school or to the same extent in all schools.[1]

It is clear that the librarian alone cannot force change. The support and commitment of administrators and of teachers is absolutely essential. Streatfield and Markless go further stating that 'school ethos will determine that school's needs for library services, and the librarian who does not take cognisance of needs and demands is likely to feel guilty and to achieve low job satisfaction.'

---

1 Haycock, Ken (1990. Services of school resource centres: a planning guide. In Haycock, K. The School Library Program in the curriculum. Englewood, CO Libraries Unlimited, p34.

Models of school library media programmes

Taxonomy one
Source: Loertscher, David V (1988). Taxonomies of the School Library Media Program. Englewood, Co: Libraries Unlimited.

Solid warehousing support

Stage one
No involvement. The library media centre is bypassed entirely. Teachers who are experienced often collect their own specialised materials or rely completely on the text. Avoidance is an habitual pattern for most students and teachers.

Stage two
Self-help warehouse. Facilities and materials are available for the self-starter (but may not be well organised). An upper level of this might include an attractive facility, with some organisational scheme. Services at this stage are the kind that no-one notices when they are running smoothly, but everyone complains about it when things go wrong. Collections grow with old out-of-date resources.

Direct services to teachers and students

Stage three
Individual reference assistance. Students or teachers get requested information or materials for specific needs. Here the library media specialist assumes the magician's role – the ability to know where to locate important and trivial information from an array of sources. Classes parade in on a schedule to learn skills that have no relevance to their classroom work. The teacher (role model for the children) often flees but rarely if ever shares any information with the librarian. Student abilities and interests remain a mystery, even though the librarian tries (is expected) to make reading suggestions.

Stage four
Spontaneous interaction and gathering. Spur-of-the-moment activities and gathering of materials occur with no advance notice. This is the level of the instant project, sudden inspiration, or new direction. It lacks cohesion on a long-term basis, and often leads collection development astray (buy for the possibility that it may happen again next year – which it never does).

Stage five

Cursory planning. Informal and brief planning with teachers and students for library media centre involvement. This is the informal-contact stage. Library acts as a clearing-house of ideas and suggestions for teachers' units and student assignments. Usually teachers insist erroneously that students will require no assistance.

Stage six

Planned gatherings. Gatherings of materials are done in advance of the class project with involvement of teacher. Lead-time allows for resources to meet all levels of ability, as well as acquiring knowledge of area resources to fall back on, if needed. Teacher discusses student interests and abilities with librarian. Scheduled classes may still be happening, but classes drop in for additional time. Still little or no connection with the regularly scheduled periods.

Stage seven

Evangelistic outreach. A concerted effort is made to promote the multimedia individualised instructional potential of the library. This includes in-service for staff, special collections of resources that are 'new' ideas. Making classroom connections, seeing that teachers really do plan joint activities, and a more flexible schedule of use begins, based on intense periods of need. Instructional objectives determine the schedule of classes in the library.

Resource based teaching

Stage eight

Scheduled planning in the support role. Formal planning is done with teachers and students. Previous instruction is reviewed so students do not have the same lesson repeated over and over again. Librarian is curriculum team member as well as a team member with the teacher. All instruction falls into a sequence that moves the student along. Instruction is undertaken for understanding not simply recall.

Stage nine

Instructional design, Level I. The librarian participates in every step of the development, execution, and evaluation of an instructional unit. Librarian works with teachers to create the objectives, assembles materials, understands content, and participates in instructional process.

Stage ten

Instructional design, Level II. The library media centre staff participates in grading students (process and research abilities) and feels an equal responsibility for their achievement.

Stage eleven

Curriculum development. Along with other educators, the librarian contributes to the planning and structure of what will actually be taught in the school or district.

Taxonomy two

Source: Haycock, Ken (1990). Services of school resource centers: a planning guide. In Haycock, K (comp). The School Library Program in the *Curriculum*. Englewood, CO: Libraries Unlimited.

Phase I – Curriculum support

Administration of resource center
Selection of materials
Acquisition of materials
Organization of materials
Circulation of materials

Phase II – Curriculum enrichment

Production of materials and services
Guidance for readers, listeners, viewers
Information services
Design and production of materials
Cooperation with outside agencies

Phase III – Curriculum implementation

Curriculum planning and involvement
Cooperative programme planning and team teaching
Professional development services to teachers

Taxonomy three

Source: Turner, Philip (1885). Helping Teachers Teach. Littleton, Colorado. Libraries Unlimited.

Level I No involvement

Perhaps no intervention is required; teacher may not have requested intervention; librarian/ media specialist (LMS) may be unwilling or unable to intervene.

Level 2 – Passive participation

Little or no interaction between LMS and teacher; LMS selects and maintains the resources which the teacher will use.

Level 3 – Reaction

Teacher may require random and inconsequential assistance of the (LMS); not part of a structured, developmental programme.

Level 4 – Action education

Nearest to formal instructional design as postulated. LMS is part of a team in the instructional process; LMS might in-service staff; helps improve curriculum delivery.

Taxonomy Four

Source: Streatfield, David and Markless, Sharon (1994) Invisible Learning? *The Contribution of School Libraries to Teaching and Learning*. Report to the British Library Research and Development Department on the 'Effective School Library' Research Project, Library and Information Research Report, 98. Boston Spa: British Library Research and Development Department.
The library programme by phases of school development

Traditional / Didactic

Teaching style	emphasis on teaching
Topic work	teacher-controlled, does not involve librarian
Teacher involvement with library	minimal (except in English); fiction reading
Programmes of study	Unlikely to refer to books/ learning resources
Teacher expectation of librarian	Book clerk
Teacher view of library	Book store
Student involvement	Constrained; may ask librarian where things are
Type of library role preferred	'Fiction'

Nominally flexible

Teaching style	Teaching and some 'independent work'
Topic work	Theme notified to librarian - specific resources requested
Teacher involvement with library	Source of information and materials
Programmes of study	Unlikely to refer to library
Teacher expectation of librarian	'Obliging'
Teacher view of library	'A good thing'
Student involvement	Sent to use; may ask librarian answers to questions set by teachers or for help
Type of library role preferred	'Lending'

Developmental

Teaching style	Mix of teaching / projects / assignments
Topic work	Theme + approach discussed with librarian + support requested
Teacher involvement with library	Source of support and help
Programmes of study	They may refer to the library; librarian may receive copies
Teacher expectation of librarian	Useful, supportive
Teacher view of library	Use important for children
Student involvement	Brought to use; may ask librarian for help when stuck
Type of library role preferred	'Physical access'

Resource based

Teaching style	Emphasis on learning
Topic work	Planned + delivered with librarian
Teacher involvement with library	Central to learning
Programmes of study	Negotiated with librarian. who receives copies; systematic reference to the library as a resource
Teacher expectation of librarian	Colleague and ally
Teacher view of library	Resource important for learning
Student involvement	Independent working; sees librarian as point of access beyond library
Type of library role preferred	'Intellectual access'

Appendix H

Selection, Acquisition, and Access

Supporting policies and documents

Samples of policies and procedures included in this section:
- Internet Related Policies & Procedures
- Challenged Materials
- Computer Software Policy
- Internet Contract
- Student Acceptable Use Policy Registration Form
- Employee Acceptable Use Policy Registration Form
- Library Bill of Rights – American Library Association
- The Freedom to Read Statement – American Library Association
- Access to Resources and Services in the School Library Media Program: an Interpretation of the ALA Library Bill of Rights – American Association of School Librarians
- Statement on Confidentiality of Library Records – American Association of School Librarians
- Statement on Intellectual Freedom – Association for Educational Communications and Technology
- IFLA Position paper on copyright in the electronic environment
- Bellingham Public Schools Policy Documents

The documents listed above can be viewed/downloaded from the ECIS web site <www.ecis.org/libraries> or you will find links to the originating site.

Internet related policies & procedures

There are several aspects to using the Internet that require some serious thought by the school. Jamieson McKenzie at Bellingham (WA) Public Schools has developed the most thoughtful and comprehensive examples of policies and procedures. The rationale behind these documents can be found on his Web site <www.fromnowon.org> which is a must for referral for anyone initiating or assessing recently prepared school documents. He advocates the necessity of developing a Board Policy, Parents Permission letters, and both Student and Staff Access Agreements. Examples of all of these documents can be found at <www.bham.wednet.edu>

Board policy and procedures

Board policies describe acceptable student behaviours, echoing the content of AUPs, connect those to existing policies on student rights and responsibilities, and tie consequences and procedures to those already in effect. In addition, it takes a position on access to potentially controversial information, connecting them to existing selection of resources policies (sample Selection, Acquisition, and Access policy is in the Appendix).

Acceptable use policies

There are several considerations to be taken into account when constructing an Acceptable Use Policy. First is that it applies to both the students body and the school staff. Inappropriate behaviour on the part of either must be handled by both due process and disciplinary procedures. While one normally assumes that students will be asked to sign such a policy, more and more schools are finding that it is wise to have students and staff follow established guidelines in accessing or posting information on the Web. Students or staff who choose not to sign an AUP can be restricted to the school Intranet, or allowed to use the Internet only under strict supervision. Many policies include details of what is acceptable use and what is unacceptable so students have a more concrete understanding of what is unacceptable behaviour. These often include visiting and/or downloading inappropriate (defined?) materials or graphics, posting to inappropriate news groups, mass mailings (spam), inappropriate downloading of files (again, defined?), sending inappropriate mail (flaming), violating copyright laws. This latter is both difficult to interpret and to police. However, it should be remembered that any and all information, including graphics, on the Internet is subject to copyright law. It is not exempt, nor is the ownership abrogated by not putting a copyright symbol on the material.

AUP content should include:

Overview: The philosophy of the school and its governing body regarding the school's provision of access to the Internet and World Wide Web (www) and its value to the educational process is the subject of this section. The policy of the governing body regarding the rationale for making available the hardware, networks, intranets, *etc.* should be made clear.

Introduction: This section explores the many capabilities and responsibilities of the use of this powerful tool as a privilege. The intent of use of for educational pursuits, and other uses are inappropriate and that ignoring this intent will bring about appropriate sanctions.

Moral and ethical issues: This section intends to explain the etiquette to be observed as part of this global community. It reaffirms the curriculum support purpose of access, and while acknowledging the existence of inappropriate information, explains that the school cannot guarantee that any combination of software, hardware, or vigilance will completely control all of the unacceptable materials which students may access. It may also discuss the possible use of blocking software

Parental notfication and responsibilty: While parents own the primary responsibility for transmitting any particular set of family values to their children, this section notes that the school will encourage parents to specify to their children what material is and is not acceptable for their child(ren) to access through the Internet and www.

E-mail accounts: If students are provided with individual e-mail accounts, an agreement will be required which must be signed by both student and parent will be provided in this section.

Electronic field trips: Parental permission slips, the same as required for other school field trips would be required for access to an electronic field trip. This section would include such a statement.

Electronic libraries: The school's selection, acquisition, and access policy will provide the substance for this section of the AUP. Information that does not meet the criteria set forth by the policy will not be approved for use in the curriculum.

Using the resources: This section defines the courteous behaviour expected of students as they work on the Internet and www within their classes and the library.

Limits of liability: The school may wish to set forth its responsibilities, either expressed or implied, that the function of the network will be error-free or without defect. This section will need to conform to the legalities of each school setting.

Expected behaviour: This section discusses safety issues, avoidance of harassment, privacy issues and, in general, cautions students and staff about the careful use of the Internet and www. Appropriate language, respect for privacy of others, and respecting the resource limits of the school (clearing email storage, subscribe to high quality listserves, *etc* are noted here.

Due process: The steps that the school follows in the event of a compromising situation, *eg* co-operating fully with local, state, or federal authorities, and the disciplinary procedures that will be followed in the event of a problem.

Mounting www sites: The process and procedure of mounting web pages, connected to the school main www site, and identifying same as to correct source is explained. The particular dangers of mounting copyrighted (or plagiarised) materials may be included here.

Challenged materials – request for reconsideration of a book and/or other instructional materials

Please check type of material:

Book ☐   Video ☐   Kit ☐   Magazine ☐

Cassette ☐   Website ☐   Pamphlet ☐   Record ☐

Other (specify) ....

Author ....
Title ....
Publisher (if known) ....
Request initiated by ....
Telephone ....
Address ....

Complainant represents:
Self ....
(Name of Organization) ....
(Identify other group) ....

1 To what in the material do you object? Please specify; cite pages and/or examples:
2 What do you feel might be the result of reading or using this material?
3 For what age group do you recommend this material?
4 Is there anything good about this material?
5 Did you read and/or review all the material? What parts?
6 Are you aware of the judgement of this material by literary critics?
7 What do you believe is the theme of this material?
8 What would you like your school to do about this material?
   Do not assign it to my child ☐
   Withdraw it from all students as well as from my child ☐
   Send it for reconsideration ☐
9 In its place, what material of equal literary quality would recommend that would convey as valuable a picture and perspective of our civilization?

Signature of complainant ....

Computer software copyright regulations

It is the intent of the.................................... School to adhere to the provisions of international copyright laws that apply to microcomputer
A. The legal, ethical, and practical problems caused by software piracy will be taught as a part of the educational technology and library information programme in the school.

B. All employees of the....................................School are expected to adhere to the provisions of these international copyright agreements to allow for the making of a backup copy or computer programs.
    1 That such a new copy of adaptation is created as an essential step in the utilisation of the computer programme in conjunction with a machine and that it is used in no other manner, or
    2 that such a new copy and adaptation is for archival purposes only and that all archival copies are destroyed in the event that continued possession of the computer programme should cease to be rightful.

C. When copyrighted software is to be used on a computer network, efforts will be made to secure this software from unauthorised copying.

D Illegal copies of copyrighted programmes may not be made or used on computing equipment owned by the....................................School.

E. It is the policy of the....................................School that there shall be no duplication of copyrighted or proprietary programmes on computers belonging to the....................................Schools and that such hardware shall be affixed with a permanent sign that contains this restriction.

F. The Head of the School, or his designee, are the only individuals who may sign school software licensing agreements.

G. No employee of the school shall access surreptitiously or illegally any database or electronic bulletin board.

H. No employee of the school shall encourage or allow any student to surreptitiously or illegally access any database or electronic bulletin board.

I. The principal of each building is responsible for establishing practices that will uphold this policy at the building level.

Adapted from the Lowell Schools Computer Software Policy, with permission.

Internet contract

Between..(school)

and ....(student)

I, the undersigned, agree to observe the following conditions while using the school's Internet Account.

I will indicate the start and end time of each Internet session using the logbook on the circulation desk.

Access to the Internet is personal and non-transferrable. I will respect the confidentiality of the Internet Access Password and will not share it with any student who is not authorised to use the school Internet account, nor will I perform Internet searches on the behalf of any student who has not attended the Internet Training Sessions.

I will not attempt to alter the settings of the hardware or software, or tamper in any way with the computer set-up, including changing the password or connection protocol. Any problems encountered during this session should be reported immediately to the librarian.

I will properly log on and off, making sure that the modem has been disconnected at the end of each session.

In keeping with the philosophy of the school, I will not access materials, which are inappropriate. Specifically, texts and graphics containing pornography, obscenity, racist, sexist, or other inappropriate characteristics may not be accessed on the school account. If in doubt, ask the librarian.

Violations of this clause will result in permanent revocation of Internet rights.

Access to the Web may or may not include e-mail privileges. However, responding to web pages requesting e-mail is not to be done. E-mail accounts are reserved for official school business only.

Access is on a first-come, first-serve basis. Sessions may be limited to one-half hour; class activities may pre-empt individual use.

Online games may not be played on school computers.

I understand that the conditions of this contract may change at any time. I also understand that by violating any of the prescriptions outlined above may curtail or revoke my computer privileges permanently.

I agree with the conditions as outlined above and will use the Internet in a manner that reflects well upon me and the school.

Signature.. Date...

Adapted from the Internet Contract from St John's International School, Waterloo, Belgium

Student acceptable use policy registration form

I have read the (*name of school*) Student Acceptable Use policy for the Internet and the World Wide Web, and agree to use these resources in accordance thereof.

Further, my parent(s) or guardian(s) and I have been advised that the (name of school) does not have control of the information on the Internet or the World Wide Web, which may contain material that is potentially offensive to some people. It is the (name of school) intent to make Internet and www access available to further educational goals and objectives.

The (*name of school*) believes that the benefits to educators and students from access to the Internet and www, in the form of information resources and opportunities for collaboration, far exceed any disadvantages of access. But ultimately, the parent(s) or guardian(s) of minors are responsible for setting and conveying the standards that their child(ren) should follow. To that end, the (name of school) supports and respects each family's right to decide whether or not to allow their child(ren) to utilise the resources of the Internet and www.

The student and her/his parent(s) or guardian(s) shall understand that student access to the Internet and www is being provided in support of the (name of school)'s educational programme. The specific conditions and services being offered will change from time to time. In addition, (name of school) makes no warranties with respect to (name of school) School Wide Area Network and Internet, www service, and it specifically assumes no responsibility for:

A. The content of any advice or information received by a student from a source outside the school, or any costs or charges incurred as a result of seeing or accepting such advice;
B. Any costs, liability or damages caused by the way the student chooses to use her/his Internet, www access;
C. Any consequences of service interruptions or changes, even if these disruptions arise from circumstances under the control of the Information Technology Department.

Student name (signature) ....
Print name ....Grade level........................
Date..

Employee acceptable use policy registration use form

Name..

Position..

Department..

I have read (name of school)'s Employee Acceptable Use Policy. I agree to follow the rules contained in this policy. I understand that if I violate the rules, I may face disciplinary action in accord with the due process in the manner set forth in the disciplinary code(s) of the school.

I hereby release (name of school), their personnel, and any institutions with which they are affiliated, from any and all claims and damages of any nature arising from any use of, or inability to use, the Internet and/or World Wide Web resources.

Signature .... Date................................

This document is based on the form in The Student's Right to Read published by the National Council of Teachers of English, USA.

Appendix I

Adjacencies

As the library programme plan evolves, it carries with it space requirements. The activities in large part determine how the floor plan evolves. They also contribute to the decision on how much space is needed, how many students or staff will be accommodated, *etc.* A sample 'adjacency zones' plan (Fig.1) is shown to provide a visual map of what this phase of facilities design involves.

What activities should be planned to be near the entrance of the center?

What activities require close proximities?

What programme activities require students to move between one area and another?

How is noise accommodated? Activities that generate physical movement of students, or sharing information will need to be placed away from areas of quiet study.

Programme activities requiring electrical power should be planned with wall adjacencies, if possible. Floor outlets are never where they should be!

What sight lines are required between adjacent activities?

These and other questions are addressed as one thinks through the process of developing an adjacency plan.

Adjacencies

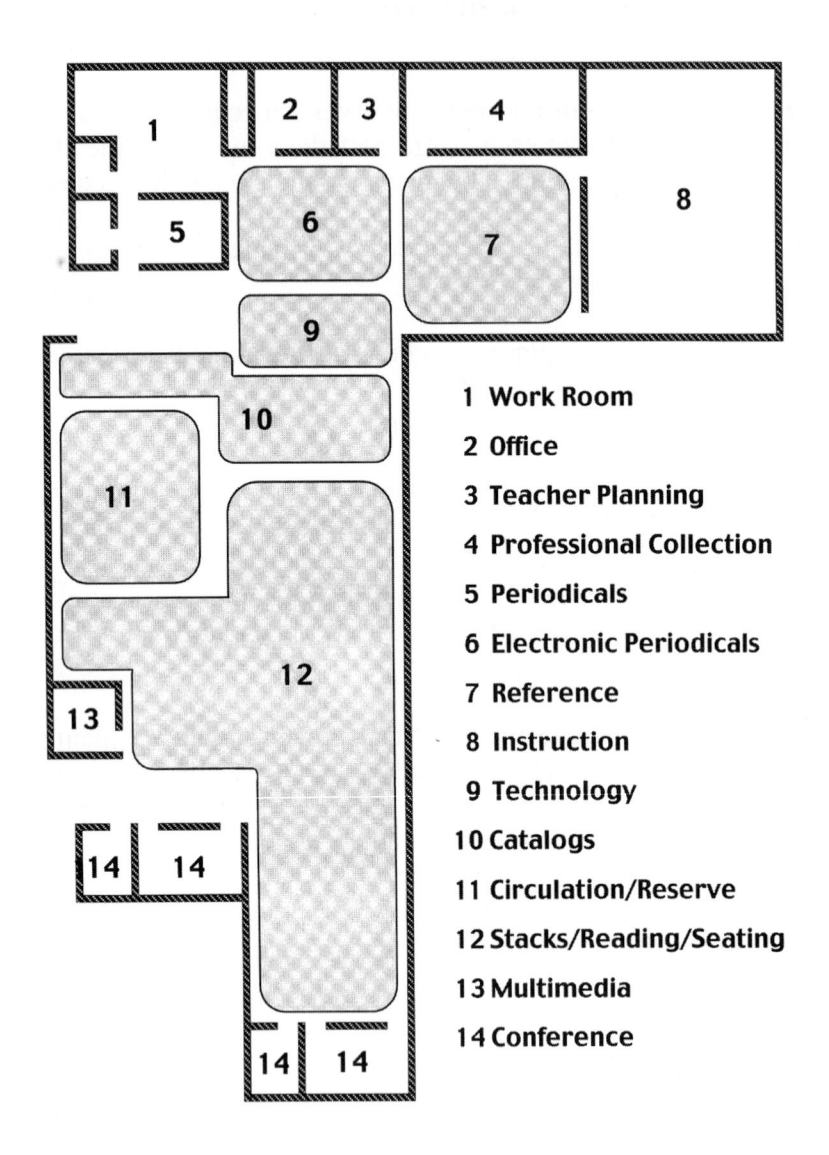

1 Work Room
2 Office
3 Teacher Planning
4 Professional Collection
5 Periodicals
6 Electronic Periodicals
7 Reference
8 Instruction
9 Technology
10 Catalogs
11 Circulation/Reserve
12 Stacks/Reading/Seating
13 Multimedia
14 Conference

Fig.1 Adjacency Plan

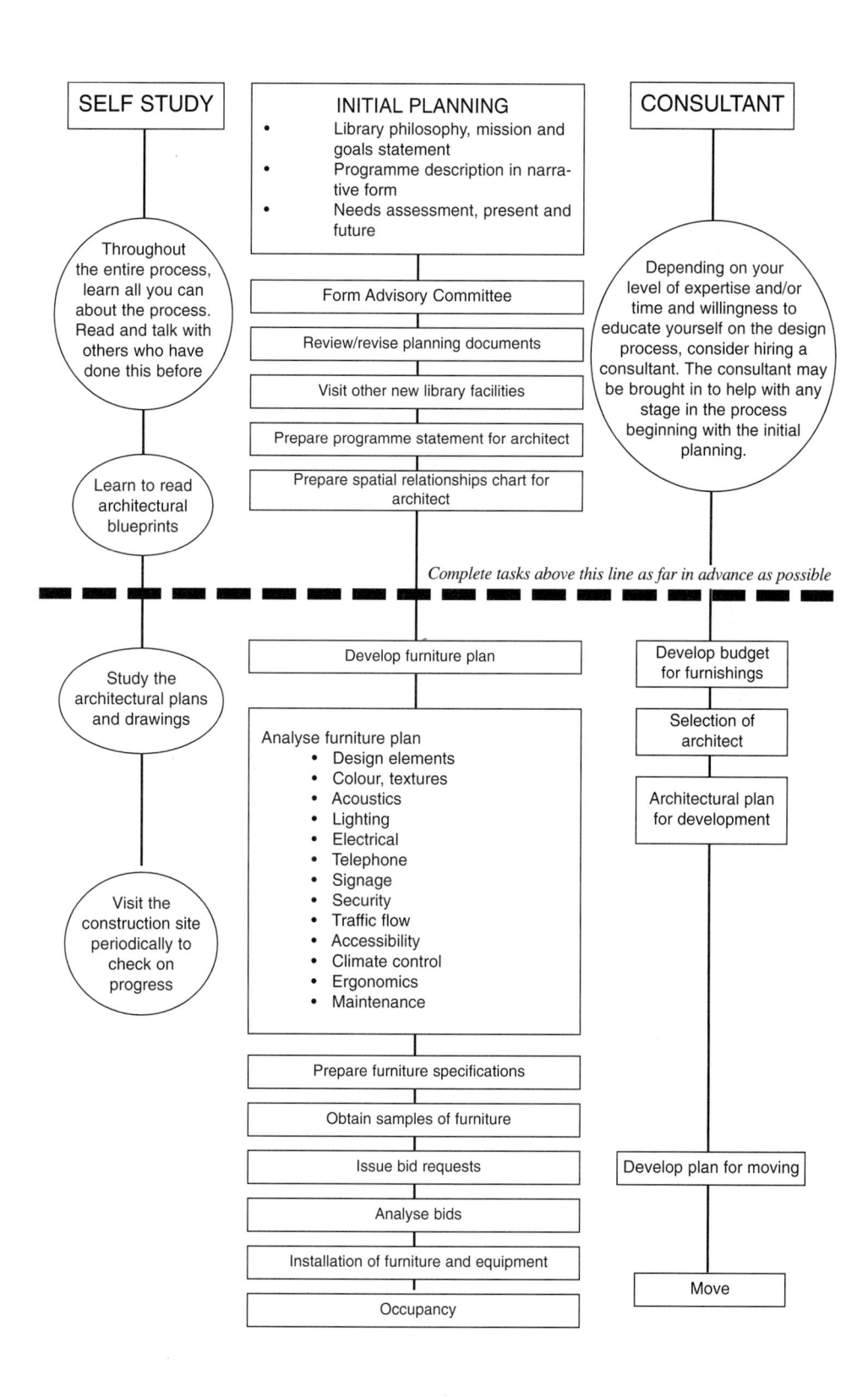

Adjacencies

SELF STUDY

(Throughout the entire process, learn all you can about the process. Read and talk with others who have done this before)

(Learn to read architectural blueprints)

— — — — — — — — — — — — — — — — — — — —

(Study the architectural plans and drawings)

(Visit the construction site periodically to check on progress)

INITIAL PLANNING

- Library philosophy, mission and goals statement
- Programme description in narrative form
- Needs assessment, present and future

- Form Advisory Committee
- Review/revise planning documents
- Visit other new library facilities
- Prepare programme statement for architect
- Prepare spatial relationships chart for architect

Complete tasks above this line as far in advance as possible

- Develop furniture plan

- Analyse furniture plan
  - Design elements
  - Colour, textures
  - Acoustics
  - Lighting
  - Electrical
  - Telephone
  - Signage
  - Security
  - Traffic flow
  - Accessibility
  - Climate control
  - Ergonomics
  - Maintenance

- Prepare furniture specifications
- Obtain samples of furniture
- Issue bid requests
- Analyse bids
- Installation of furniture and equipment
- Occupancy

CONSULTANT

(Depending on your level of expertise and/or time and willingness to educate yourself on the design process, consider hiring a consultant. The consultant may be brought in to help with any stage in the process beginning with the initial planning.)

- Develop budget for furnishings
- Selection of architect
- Architectural plan for development

- Develop plan for moving
- Move

Appendix J

Library Professionals

Librarian competencies

In the spring of 1998, the New England Educational Media Association initiated a process that identified the criteria and indicators that define the competencies the school librarian / library media specialist should possess. This was a suggested outcome of a training session for evaluation team chairs for the New England Association of Schools and Colleges. The competencies are focused on the teaching and learning process as carried out in the library media programme.

The School Library Media Specialist understands, promotes, and can provide evidence to support the fact that:

>Information Literacy is an integral part of the curriculum.
>Collaborative planning and teaching between the librarian and classroom teachers is the norm rather than the exception.
>Resource based learning experiences and environments are the foundation of the educational and instructional process.
>Literatures, in all formats, are valid, valuable bases for learning in all subject areas, and a robust collection of resources has been developed to achieve this.
>Technology is used as a tool or resource to facilitate student learning.
>The library staff continues to seize opportunities for professional growth and development.
>The resources are organised, managed, and easily accessible to students, faculty, and the school community.
>An advocacy programme that communicates the role of the library to the educational and parent community is strong and productive.
>Ethical use of ideas and information is fostered at every turn.

Sample job descriptions

While many job descriptions can be drawn from the competency statements in the manual, sample descriptions have been provided to assist the school in choosing candidates who can succeed in the role envisioned.

Head of libraries/information programme

The head of the library and/or information programme is an educational leader within the school. Sometimes the Head and the Librarian roles are combined in one person. This will depend upon the size of the school and the sophistication of the library responsibilities, the information programme, and the overall philosophy and culture of the school.

Duties of the Head Librarian or Department Head would include, but are not limited to the following:

Develops and implements an effective plan for providing a library media programme that promotes the philosophy, goals, objectives, and teaching/learning strategies of the school.

Co-ordinates the library information programme with the curriculum, budget, staff development activities, facility design and use, and media production.

Develops a budget plan based on the overall plan of the library programme.

Actively participates in the full life of the school, *eg* on curriculum committees, facility planning, personnel staffing, budget and management committees, as well as on administrative level teams.

Promotes adherence to copyright and intellectual property rights, and advocates the principles of intellectual freedom.

Encourages integration of instructional technologies to enhance learning.

Develops policies and procedures that assures the library works in concert with the educational philosophy of the school.

Has a commitment to continued learning and personal/professional growth along with intellectual curiosity.

Fosters the development of an exemplary library information literacy programme that meets or exceeds professional guidelines and standards.

Has effective problem-solving, human relations, and interpersonal communication skills.

Has a working knowledge of child development, teaching strategies, learning styles, and adult learning preferences, including recent information on multiple intelligences, brain research, cognitive development, *etc.*

Has an understanding of the school budgeting process and procedures and fiscal accountability.

Able to lead, organise, direct, and supervise the work of other staff members to meet the established goals and objectives of the programme. Participates in the life of the school.

Conducts systematic evaluations of the effectiveness of the library media instructional programme and organisational/management activities.

Understands the role of technology in today's and tomorrow's information systems.

Works co-operatively with all areas of the school programme.

Promotes the integration of information literacy skills in the teaching activities of the classroom.

Consults with teachers and administrators on the development of a resource base for their educational programme.

Establishes and maintains a welcoming atmosphere in an aesthetically pleasing environment that is conducive to productive work with students.

Create and promote an active public relations programme that keeps colleagues abreast of new trends, acquisitions, and activities.

Liase with external agencies, professional groups, organisations, *etc.* to provide a rich educational environment for the students and faculty of the school.

Librarian or library media specialist

The basic role of the library media specialist is to provide leadership for the library and information programme in the school. Under this fundamental role fall three categories: instruction, consulting, and management. Of paramount importance is the instructional role in which students are taught to locate, access, evaluate, synthesise and ultimately use the 'information' they gather to create new knowledge. This is often referred to as 'information literacy.'

The second role, that of consultant, is intended to assist the faculty in their efforts to provide quality resources appropriate to their instructional programmes. And, lastly, the library media specialist has responsibility as a programme manager – selecting, organising, and recommending for purchase a high quality body of resources, identifying appropriate resources available through sister agencies (such as the public library or regional library system), and from the World Wide Web. These resources will assure quick and easy access to an ever expanding world of information and a literature base appropriate to the age of the students. In addition, the collection must be kept current, reflect the needs of the curriculum, and be usable in an welcoming and inviting environment in which students and faculty will work. The roles are all interrelated and the effectiveness of the instructional and consultant roles rests on an efficient and effective programme management.

Duties of the library media specialist include, but are not limited to the following:

Instructional role

Develop and teach a comprehensive information skills continuum and instructional programme, ideally, connected to and/or embedded in classroom instruction and using appropriate teaching strategies. Focus instruction on concepts of information searching and the intellectual techniques rather than the mechanics of hardware or only on the specific tools available.

Understand current assessment techniques to evaluate student progress on the information skills curriculum.

Assist students in the research process. Encourage the use of research models, such as Eisenberg's Big Six, Kuhlthau, or other similar model used by the school.

Develop resources to assist students in the use of library and information resources, from bulletin boards to quick-entry helps, *etc.*

Teach students appropriate source identification via a school-wide agreed upon model of citation. Incorporate note-taking, note reconstruction, and resource evaluation in everyday instruction.

Conduct book talks and reading groups on both literature and research materials to assist students in broadening their knowledge base, making wise and appropriate selections of reading resources, *etc.*

Connect and collaborate with the public library on issues of common concern, including shared collection development.

Consultant role

Participate on curriculum development teams to provide information in support of their efforts, This involves not only identifying resources appropriate to their needs, but also professional resources through electronic searches for background information of importance for their work.

Develop regular communications programmes to keep faculty informed, solicit suggestions, and provide the library with a visible presence in the classroom. Outreach efforts in the form of newsletters, information updates *etc*, as well as informal correspondence and communications with individual faculty members and administration are routine.

Prepare bibliographies, webographies, and other resources to assist the faculty and students.

Participate in the overall life of the school community.

Management role

Set yearly goals and objectives, including year end review and evaluation of progress. Establish a linkage between management goals and instructional outcomes.

Ability to establish an action plan for the development of the collection, policies and procedures, staff and volunteer training. This plan would identify major and minor areas of development and include expected programmatic outcomes as a result of the plan.

Conduct programme assessment identifying strengths and weaknesses, with a plan for improvement.

Develop a collection of resources appropriate to the grade level of the students, the needs of the faculty, and the educational strategies and programme of the school.

Establish patterns of use for the facility which will encourage students to feel welcome at all times, able to work independently, and allow for simultaneous use by individuals, groups, and classes.

Develop a budget document that is a fiscal expression of the programme, Identify what will be needed and how it supports the programme of services for students and teachers.

Develop an acquisition programme with the assistance of the business manager for the efficient purchase of resources.

Develop a folio of policies and procedures articulating the manner in which the library media centre will function. This management manual (table of contents appended) serves as a guide for volunteers or student assistants, as a resource for the clerical support, and, in modified form, as an orientation framework for new faculty orientation.

Establish a schedule of policy and procedure reviews to assure close agreement with the mission, goals, and objectives of the school.

Use the automation system as a tool for managing the library, as a tool for learning, and as an organisational tool. Statistics on usage, adequacy of areas of the collection, currency, general inventory *etc.* all contribute to the evaluation of programme effectiveness.

Keep automated card catalogue/circulation software current and accurate. Update electronic resources to maintain currency.

Define, direct, and supervise routine clerical and volunteer assistance.

Remove from the collection old, obsolete, and inappropriate materials.

Personal role

Seek professional growth opportunities, *eg* seminars, workshops, courses, training, *etc.* both in those offered for the faculty and those specific to the school library profession, in order to keep abreast of the changes inherent in the field as they apply to the educational community.

Read extensively in the literature of the age groups served.

Demonstrates effective interpersonal skills with all members of the school community.

Library media assistant

The role of the library media assistant is to support the work of the library media specialist. To this end, the duties are primarily determined by the activity in the centre, the overall programme goals, and the connections established for collaborative efforts. In many schools this is a paraprofessional position, by the nature of the advance technological skills required; in others, it remains a clerical support position. Responsibilities include, but are not limited to:

> Circulation control, working with the automation software, CD ROMs, *etc* and providing student assistance, when requested.
> Maintaining a schedule of activities in the centre.
> Shelving used resources, or supervising student or volunteer assistance in restocking resources.
> Clerical tasks inherent in checking orders, processing resources so they are shelf-ready, checking and loading electronic records into the OPAC.
> Managing the mail and correspondence.
> Assisting the library media specialist in supervising the activities in the library media centre.
> Assisting the library media specialist in the preparation of public relations communications, memo, phone contacts, *etc*.
> Assuring the organisation of the resources is at a high level so access is efficient.
> Performing the filing, typing, communications as requested.
> Supervising the library in the absence of the library media specialist (before / after school use, if established).
> Assisting students while the librarian is unavailable or teaching.
> Assist the library media specialist in maintaining a warm and friendly environment, in which students and faculty may work and pursue their research and reading needs.
> Supports the programme by maintaining a supportive and welcoming atmosphere for all members of the school community.

Library information systems and technology paraprofessional

This position may fall under the Instructional Technology area or the Library, depending on the school's organisational structure. The goals of this position are to assist the professional staff of the school by maintaining the information and technology systems of the building. Responsibilities for this position include, but are not limited to:

> Maintaining the hardware and software, including networks in the Library Media Centre.
> Uploading, troubleshooting, and cleaning up the applications and files on the network.
> Assist in the instructional programme, informing teachers and students on the use of the centre.

Develop written documentation of the information systems.
Develop guidelines for the use of individual applications to assist students and teachers using the centre.
Assist the professional staff in maintaining an atmosphere conducive to the effective use of the facility.
Developing and maintaining a log of activities and schedule for the use of the facilities.
Learn and be able to assist students and teachers in the use of applications software.
Capable of trouble shooting and basic repairs on equipment.
Promotes the use and integration of technology in the learning environment.

Appendix K

Library Automation

Getting ready for automation

Once the decision is taken to automate the circulation and card catalogue (and other technical services processes as well), two operations will then begin in tandem. The first is to identify the characteristics you want in the software system – selecting the automation programme. The second is readying the collection for transfer from the paper trail to an electronic database. It is this second operation that is the focus of this tip sheet. A third aspect occurs as the need arises to make decisions about the required hardware and/or network requirements, *etc.*

Retroconversion

The first thing to do is to weed the collection. Deselect those resources that have taken on a shelf life of their very own... never leaving the shelf for use by students or teachers. While non-circulation for a ten-year period is pretty good evidence that the resource is no longer used, the Deselection Guidelines in this manual may help clarify what should go and what should be kept.

Some pundits who have been down this path before will tell you that the second thing you do is weed the collection again (!) on the off-chance that you just didn't have the heart to trim out the unused, misleading, erroneous, or obsolete materials on the first run through the collection.

At this point a thorough and accurate inventory of all resources to be retroconverted needs to be accomplished.

While this weeding process is proceeding, decisions need to be made as to the comprehensiveness of the database. Will only library materials be entered? What is to be done with media, hardware, texts, classroom collections, *etc*? Many schools are moving toward using the automation systems as inventory control systems and many of the software packages accommodate this without affecting the integrity of the 'library collection'.

This leads to the obvious question of how will the retroconversion be accomplished? In house? By an independent company? By the software vendor? By other means? After (or, sometimes, while) this is going on, decisions need to be made as to what kinds of records are available for the retroconversion: do they need to be created or has a 'shelf-list' been maintained by the school with the appropriate information noted? Some schools have excellent shelf-lists; others hand write cards; still others send in lists of resources. Needless to say, the more complete the record send, the higher the chance that an exact match will be made in the electronic format. Since the quality of the database in large measure determines the quality of the access to the collection, it is important to strive for best possible records. Multiple copies need to be noted; special information, such as donations or gifts, may be entered in this process, usually for an additional editing fee.

Minimum information required is an accurately spelt title, author, publisher, copyright date, LC number and ISBN number. Most companies can work without the LC or ISBN numbers, but they are most convenient if they are on the cards or list.

Decisions about local call numbers need to be made in concert with the software vendor to maximise searchability of the collection for management purposes. For example, if you want all media to sort in one list, then the call number prefix should enable this to happen; anomalies in classification schemes show up as problems unless resolved, preferably prior to the retroconversion. For example, cataloguers have vacillated about what to do with biographies over the years, or have changed their minds about the number of letters from the author's last name should be included in the call number. Now is the time to standardise these anomalies even though it means changing spine labels in the future.

Decisions on barcodes also need to be made. Are smart barcodes (barcode with classification numbers, author, title, and ownership [school name]) desired? Or will the school use pre-printed dumb barcodes that include only the ownership and barcode number? Also, the barcode standard needs to be decided. Two prevalent norms are Code 3 of 9 and Codabar. A decision now needs to be made about the length of the barcode number and whether it should include a check digit.

The two prevalent standards are a nine digit number which allows up to 999,999,999 items to be included and a 14 digit barcode that begins with a 2 (Patron) or a 3 (Resource). This is followed by 4 digits of the school's choice, and a 9 digit barcode number. The check digit is an arbitrary digit or symbol at the end of the barcode that simply assures the computer that the barwand read the label correctly. The four digits reserved for the school to choose often are accounting codes that distinguish the item's location or internal ownership, *eg,* a department, grant, textbook, *etc*.

As this process proceeds, it is extremely helpful for the librarian to become familiar with the MARC record format. MARC provides an international standard for library database records. With new technological advances, future cataloguing can be downloaded from the www through Z39.50 technology. This can virtually eliminate original cataloguing except for local or unique items.

Hardware

Equipment specifications are best gathered from the software vendor at the time of purchase. Currently no firm guidelines exist on how to calculate the number of workstations required in the library to support the automation, in-house CD-ROM or similar information software, and electronic access to www information. Any automation plan should include at least two management workstations, one dedicated to circulation, and the other for behind-the-scenes work.

In addition, student workstations need to be provided in sufficient numbers to make access efficient and reliable. Decisions about word-processing and gaming are system or building decisions that need to be made on a total school scan and not just the library. If sufficient access to computers throughout the school is possible, then few library computers would be used for word-processing; if none are available, then library computers should have this capability for students.

Automation system collection guidelines

Selecting an automation system is not necessarily a once-in-a-lifetime decision. As the technology advances, so do the quality, versatility, and user friendliness of the automation systems we use in the school library.

Whether buying your first system, or migrating to a more powerful, newer system, the decision must be based on good information. That means discarding the notion that you can get a demo disk and make that your prime decision factor. Demo disks do well what the vendor wants to show case, and avoids even mentioning the characteristics you will want to have functioning. So, setting up strong, well-developed performance criteria is a very crucial first step in the selection process.

Today, in addition to the software performance, you want to know about the fiscal health and stability of the company producing the product. The market shakedown is still going on. Several current automation software packages are recycled failed systems that have been bought out and 'made pretty' for another market round. Some companies buy the software package and fail to support it, leaving customers in the lurch when problems arise - and problems will arise.

If you have excellent technical support and it is important to be on the cutting edge, you might want to take a chance with a new software product. Otherwise, wisdom dictates that you take the conservative path and buy something that has been on the market a few years so the bugs have all been worked out. Microsoft started a new trend in selling products that the public had to (and still is) debugging. But that might not be a route you want to chance.

Some initial questions to pose and things to do

How long, and what experience does the company have with library products?

> Many programmers think they can quickly simulate a database for library use only to find that it is a very sophisticated process and simple database formats don't work well. Writing software for mainframe computers (those old things, where storage was very expensive!) is different from writing for PC or Mac-based client-server systems. Graphic interfaces, called GUIs, are the norm today, helping the systems become more user friendly and intuitive.

What is the installed base of clients for the software?

> If only a few copies have been sold, or none are in your area, there may be a minimal level of support when you need it.

How does the company envision its future?

> Once the market is saturated and everyone is electronic, what then?

Is the library software its primary concern? Or is it a convenient add-on to another product that it wants to sell?

> This could mean that little research and development money will be spent keeping this product robust and current since the companies main concern (and major revenue) is elsewhere.

Have you talked to other clients using this software?

> Many will give you honest assessments, joys as well as tribulations. If a company won't share information on other clients, say goodbye!

What kind of support line do they have?

> Does the company regularly sponsor training seminars or send knowledgeable staff around to visit? Is there a phone number you can call without excessive cost or time inconveniences? Can they manage technical support via modem lines and how much does this all add to the yearly maintenance and license fee? Also, be aware that all yearly support fees do not include routine updates or new versions of the software. This can be a shock, so ask in advance what the company's policy is regarding new versions and/or upgrades of the software.

Does it accept the standard MARC record?

> This is important if you want to purchase your materials already processed and shelf ready - a real time saver. Can you add other databases into the software and have them treated as if they were MARC format? This is handy if you have a specialised database developed in-house that you want to fold into the automation system.

Get referees and call them.

> Ask if they were buying today, would they make the same choice? Ask what they see as the strengths and weaknesses of the product. If they see no weaknesses, probe to see if their use would not demand the sophistication that your use would require (*eg* how does it handle reserve

materials? or add an item 'on the spot' that someone needs immediately; can you add other locations on campus and at what cost?).

Develop a list of characteristics

Develop a list of characteristics that the software MUST have and ask each vendor to demonstrate its capability.

Check if the software runs well on a network.

If stand-alone products are buggy, wait until they are thrown up on a network! They may bring the network down because of some programming quirk. Hopefully this problem is now solved, but it was a big one a few years ago.

Professional evaluations in the literature are of little help.

Software moves on; publishing takes time! Often the system you are seeing is not the one evaluated. Also, some of the evaluators have difficulty controlling their own biases and ask different questions of their favourites. Others apply mainframe criteria to PC-based systems – also a problem.

Think about the add-on costs that accrue.

For example, does the company do its own retrospective conversions or farm them out to others? Find out where and who is doing it, how large the database that is being used is, and what the cost is, particularly for customisation. Standard fees should include simple editing, local call numbers, and the like. Have the vendor price out the software without and with the retrospective conversion. Some 'so-called' bargains disappear when the set-up and editing fees begin to mount. Choices are available with some companies employing college students while others use trained library personnel. The best automation system cannot improve a deficient or inaccurate database.

Check out the printing (report) versatility.

This is one of the more complicated aspects of the software and, if done well, is well worth the money it adds to the software package. Remember that schools have different report needs than public or academic libraries. One software package could not limit the overdues by date or teacher or homeroom. Every week the library spent a day cutting and pasting, putting together the lists for a classroom!

Request that the companies you are targeting provide you with a 'bid specification' packet.

Every characteristic of the software will be identified. Compare those you are requiring or considering.

Visit someone who has the programme up and running.

The best information is to see the product in operation. One system I have heard of gets glowing reviews in the media, and from clients, yet when seen in operation, was so slow that the circulation desk had to install a second computer just to check out books to a class of children during a normal visit period.

Don't let your ego get tied up in this decision!

Every situation has different twists and peculiarities so someone else's choice may not be your best answer. As the technology improved, so did the capabilities of the PC – based systems.

Today's systems do not require you to compromise on user friendliness or ease of use for young children. The market is sufficiently robust that there are good choices out there waiting for clients!

A checklist of automation criteria for purposes of comparison

Accepts locally developed databases	Keyword and Boolean searches
Accepts partial inventories	Media booking module
Acquisition module	Modem mail merge
Authority control (assures consistency in author names, geographical spellings, *etc*)	Multilingual search screens
	Multi-phase data entry
Automatically eliminates 'a', 'an', and 'the' from initial word in title	On-screen help
	On-screen messaging
Browse keywords – turn on or off specific words	Patron fields include sufficient space for names and phones
Bulletin board capability (notices to students, staff, *etc*)	Patron module links to and/or accepts records from the school database of students
Can be www mounted	
Can design own reports	Quick response time with large database and full network operating
Can print barcodes and spine labels	
Circulation using either barcode or person's name (alpha-characters)	Rebuild keyword index
	Remote access
Company fiscal stability	Runs some CD-ROMs using OPAC* screens As separate software packages As single search (one search finds all)
Confidentiality of records	
Create bibliographies with/without annotations; choose arrangement (author, Call. No. *etc*)	
	Save searches
Create reserves	School owns the database
Creates overdue lists, notices, parent letters	Searches yield consistent responses
	Serials module
Cross references	Supports postscript printing
Dual platform (Win/Mac)	Training offered
Ease of editing	Union catalogue with circulation link
Easy entry template	Unlimited subject headings
Free phone support	Updates included in support fees
Full MARC records	Variable field lengths
Global author editing	Word-processing merge
Global delete of materials, patrons	Written documentation
Global subject editing	Z39.50 compatible
ILL connection	

* OPAC Online Public Access Catalogue – the card catalogue

Appendix L

Learning and Information
The Future

Learning and Libraries - Trends for the Future

Predicting the future is always a risky business. Yet, there are so many trends today that reinforce the fact that we educators have known since ancient times, at least as far back as Plato's era, ***how*** to teach. The arguments over the ages have been primarily over ***what*** we teach. Yet, few schools can honestly say that the ***how*** has been attended to in any rigorous manner.

Our intense information age has produced numerous studies that are beginning to craft a more clear picture of how children learn, how their minds work, and how we as educators can design 'best practice' to take advantage of nature's own pathways. This has led cognitive psychologists to better articulate to educators how to teach children to learn to learn (metacognition). For learning in this new age will, of necessity, be a lifelong endeavour. New research, new information, and new explorations are leading us into a universe of exponentially expanding knowledge. And while the speed of information continually increases, our mind's ability to absorb new information and ideas has remained relatively static over the past 3000 years.

Today, traditional classrooms are gradually yielding to a multiplicity of teaching techniques and strategies in order to engage <u>all</u> students in an active learning process. We cannot afford to leave anyone behind. The bar for the work-a-day world continues to rise higher and higher. And, while education is not solely an activity to prepare for the world of work, for educators to ignore this aspect of learning is to do so at great risk. The job market continues to tell us that not only will this new millennium require students to know and understand the basics. They will be required to collaborate with others, synthesise new information quickly, reason, persuade, express themselves in a multitude of ways, communicate in a global village effectively, and all the while understand the influence of culture on the thinking of their peers and colleagues.

Our job as librarians and teachers is to help students move forward in this information world, as literate information consumers that will be able to use both the intellectual and technical (mechanical) skills required to access and interpret the data and information they find. The role of the teacher is to mentor, coach, and provide expert guidance to use this data and information to create new knowledge and ultimately, wisdom. Traditionally, the role of the library has been to archive information in the event it would be needed. Today, the role has dramatically changed as librarians are in many ways the keeper of the keys to the efficient and effective techniques needed to manoeuvre in this mass of information.

Tomorrow, the essential role of the school librarian will be to assist the students in identifying and access *quality* information not just quantities of information, evaluate this information, and be able to make connections and develop new insights into the meaning of new knowledge. This role requires both teachers and school librarians to shift their paradigms: teachers from dispensers and synthesisers of 'all one needs to know' to orchestral conductors of new learning environments; and librarians, from passive information storage to active information laboratories where information is often accessible only in hypertext modes rather than the older traditional linear models we have been accustomed to.

This, and the intensity of graphical presentations of data to our more visually astute students, means we must also shift our ideas from concern about what format the information is taking to the quality and value of the information and data itself. We need not fear the demise of the printed book! It won't happen... at least not in the ways we fear. The concept of 'book' will remain, but it may be presented in digital formats that look and feel 'bookish' for a while. One can look at the development of the automobile and see the parallels – the earliest were carriages on wheels – a far cry from today's sleek, low slung machines; or the phone... What we are learning is that it is not the format that is critical, but the content. The decision of format (print, multimedia, video, etc) should be consistent with the integrity of the information and intent of the message and not simply an arbitrary or whimsical choice.

For example, recent releases of 1950's filmstrips in CD-ROM format do nothing to enhance the poor quality of the original production! While the interactive role of the librarian and teacher has been changing slowly since the advent of computer-based technology, the sophistication of the information base has accelerated the pace of constant collaboration. Texts were entirely adequate resources in an information scarce world; they are less and less viable in an information rich environment. Inquiry and resource based learning inherently depends on a wealth of information and resources, readily available, organised effectively, easily accessible and ready when the need demands it.

Stephen Hawkins in his *Brief History of Time* aptly describes the explosion of information in the increase in human knowledge.

> 'In Newton's time it was possible for an educated person to have a grasp of the whole human knowledge, at least in outline. But since then, the pace of the development of science has made this impossible...Only few people can keep up with the rapidly advancing frontier of knowledge,

and they have to devote their whole time to it and specialise in a small area. The rest of the population has little idea of the advances that are being made or the excitement they are generating. Seventy years ago, if Eddington is to be believed, only two people understood the theory of relativity. Nowadays tens of thousands of university graduates do...'

The international school community has a unique contribution to make to this new global information society. Building the information laboratories, staffing them appropriately, and integrating their work into routine classroom instruction will be the challenge for the millennium. It is eminently achievable, and well worth the effort for our students are our future as world citizens of the new age.

Appendix M

The Basic Bibliography - Getting Started

Allen, C. (Ed.). (1991) *Skills for Life: Library Information Literacy for Grades K-6.* (The Book Report and Library Talk Professional Growth series). Worthington, OH: Linworth.

American Association of School Librarians (1998). *Information Power: Building Partnerships for learning.* (2nd ed.) Chicago: American Association of School Librarians.

Bamford, R. A. & Christo, J. C. (eds) (1998). *Making Facts Come Alive: Choosing Quality Nonfiction Literature K-8.* Norwood, Ma: Christopher–Gordon Publishers.

Beers, K. & Samuels, B. G. (eds) (1998). *Into Focus: Understanding and Creating Middle School Readers.* Norwood, Ma: Christopher-Gordon Publishers.

Coles, M., White, C., & Brown, P. (1993). *Learning Matters: Active Approaches to Studying: A Resource for Teaching about Studying, Coursework, Revision and Exams.* Carlisle: Carel Press.

Cooling, W. (1998). *Books to Enjoy, 8 to 12.* Swindon: School Library Association.

Cooling, W. (1996). *Books to Enjoy, 12 to 16.* Swindon: School Library Association.

Cullinan, B.E. (1992). *Read to Me: Raising Kids Who Want to Read.* New York: Scholastic.

Dubber, G. (1996). *Organising Voluntary Help in the School Library* (SLA Guidelines). Swindon: School Library Association.

Eisenberg, M. & Berkowitz, R. (1988). *Curriculum Initiative: An Agenda and Strategy for Library Media Programs* (Information Management, Policy, and Services series). Norwood, NJ: Ablex Publishing Corporation.

Eisenberg, M. & Berkowitz, R. (1988). *Resource Companion for Curriculum Initiative: An Agenda and Strategy for Library Media Programs* (Information Management, Policy, and Services series). Norwood, NJ: Ablex Publishing Corporation.

Education Department of Tasmania. (1986). *Teaching Students How to Learn: Ideas for Teaching Information Skills.* (2nd ed). Tasmania: Education Department of Tasimania.

Gawith, G. (1987). *Library Alive!* London: A&C Black.

Gawith, G. (1990). *Reading Alive!* London: A&C Black.

Kibbey, M. (Ed). (1994). *Skills for Life: Library Information Literacy for Grades 6-8.* (The Book Report and Library Talk Professional Growth series). Worthington, OH: Linworth.

Lima, C.W. (1998). *A to Zoo: Subject Access to Children's Picture Books.* (5th ed) NY: Bowker.

Loertscher, D. (1998). *Reinvent Your School's Library in the Age of Technology: A Handbook for Superintendents and Principals.* Castle Rock, CO: Hi Willow Research & Pub.

Loertscher, D. (1988). *Taxonomies of the School Library Media Program.* Enlgewood CO: Libraries Unlimited.

Robertson, S (1993). *Development Planning for the School Library Resource Centre.* (SLA Guidelines). Swindon: School Library Association.

Rux, P. (ed). (1993). *Skills for Life: Library Information Literacy for Grades 9-12.* (The Book Report and Library Talk Professional Growth series). Worthington, OH: Linworth.

School Library Association (1992). *Matters of Choice: Selecting Books for the Library.* (SLA Guidelines). Swindon: School Library Association.

School Library Management Notebook (4th ed. 1998). (Professional Growth Series). Worthington, OH: Linworth.

Scott, E. & Johnstone, J (1992). *Managing Materials: Basic Routines in the School Library* (SLA Guidelines). London: School Library Association.

Tilke, A. (ed) (1998). *Guidelines for School Librarians.* London: Library Association Publishing.

Tilke, A. (1998). *On the Job Sourcebook for School Librarians.* London: Library Association Publishing.

Trelease, J (1995). *The Read-Aloud Handbook* (4th ed). Harmondsworth: Penguin.

Valenza, J K (1998). *Power Tools: 100+ Essential Forms and Presentations for your School Library Information Program.* Chicago: American Library Association.

Winkel, L. (1998) *Elementary School Library Collection* (21st ed). Williamsport, PA: Brodart.

Postscript

Dr Gray Mattern wrote the following foreword for the first edition of this publication in 1987. He clearly saw the impact that the new information world was to have on ECIS classrooms and programs. His wisdom and energy inspired many schools to rise to the challenge and move their libraries from sideline supporters to mainstream curricular involvement by direct instructional collaboration with the classroom. Thus, this edition is dedicated to his vision and in his memory.

Carolyn A Markuson, 1999

In the current wisdom about what constitutes a 'good school', one of the most frequently encountered perceptions is the central importance of the school library. Indeed, it is a significant mark of the attention that this facet of school operation is receiving that the word itself has become controversial. Some commentators insist that the word 'library' is too narrow in its connotations, suggesting simply an inert collection of books catalogued (it is hoped!) and arranged on shelves, contained in a room which every school is supposed to have somewhere, but whose function is none too clear and which is, in any case, more an institutional ornament than an essential ingredient of the educational enterprise.

To change this image, to suggest the potential of vital impact on the learning process, to alter the concept of the library from a place to a functional role in what a school is all about, the term 'learning media centre' is now used in many schools, in both North America and the United Kingdom, and, increasingly, around the anglophone world. The term has its value, too, in pointing to the fact that the resources available to support the teaching and learning process are not confined to books or printed matter, but potentially include also the whole rich cornucopia of machinery and materials resulting from sophisticated technology and affecting virtually every human sensory capacity.

Though for the most part the terms 'library' and 'librarian' are used here (because they are convenient – and occasion less risk of the faint whiff of derision emanating from such an orotundity as 'learning media centrist'), it is the purpose of the document which follows to promote an understanding and acceptance amongst international schools of this expanded role for the school library.

And it is surely time. One of the conclusions reached from visits to a great many institutions, and not alone in Europe, is that too many of them give insufficient attention to their libraries. I have seen schools in which there is no library at all as such – and have been advised that there is no necessity for one, because each teacher keeps books, which may be needed in his/her own classroom. I have seen schools in which 'the library' is a few shelves on a dark corridor, holding a pathetic collection of dog-eared paperbacks, scattered seemingly at random, unknown, unloved and unused. I have visited schools which have with special pride showed me their libraries: a room with a collection of materials - and sometimes, quite a respectable collection – neatly arranged and scrupulously catalogued, but in which nothing happens because it is clearly an irrelevance to the ongoing life of the institution. And in schools such as those described above, I have encountered 'librarians' ranging from the assigned student monitor to the occasional volunteer mother, the school nurse, a concerned teacher who can't stand it any longer, and the well-trained, full-time librarian reigning in splendid isolation from her colleagues, pupils, and anything at all to do with the educative process. Sometimes I have been offered explanations (excuses?), mostly having to do with money, but occasionally with philosophy. And sometimes there has seemed to be a total lack of awareness that there is anything missing at all or, on the contrary even a belief that indeed the library is right up to the mark, a place to be shown off with confident expectation of praise.

There are, of course, many marvellous libraries and librarians in international schools – welcoming, vital places at the hub of the teaching and learning process, staffed by bright, creative, dedicated professionals recognised by both colleagues and students as a force linking the whole of the parts of the educational experience. And all praise and credit to such persons, for they have not always achieved their positions simultaneously with their appointments. Indeed, the original inspiration for this document arose from the concerns of our own Committee on Libraries, the first ECIS Staff Service Committee and still one of the most active and hard-working standing groups, to which many talented librarians in Council schools have made distinguished contributions. It is in recognition of what the library in an international school can and ought to be, even in a small school, isolated from the most pertinent resources and with severely limited means, that this study is presented. It is the implicit conviction that no school need be without a good library. It is as well as the hope that, as a result of this exercise, no school will be.

A word, then, about what follows. Convinced of the need for an attack on the shortcomings of libraries in Council schools, particularly at the elementary level, ECIS sought the advice of one of the best known US practitioners in the field, Dr Carolyn Markuson, Supervisor of Libraries and Instructional Materials, Brookline Public Schools, Brookline, Massachusetts. Dr Markuson also had some familiarity with international schools and their peculiar problems, having served as consultant to individual institutions and having worked closely with the ECIS Committee on Libraries. With her help, a proposal was formulated and presented to the Overseas Schools Advisory Council of the Office of Overseas Schools, US Department of State, which in due course agreed to support the initial research study and the subsequent production of this manual.

Postscript

During the winter of 1987, Dr Markuson sent an extensive questionnaire to all ECIS schools, one part of which solicited responses from the chief administrative officer, the other from the librarian. Based on the results, nine pilot schools of various sizes and types were designated and, in the Autumn, were visited by Dr Markuson for the purpose of closer investigation and consultation about their library programmes. A summary of her findings from the questionnaire and the school visits, along with extensive recommendations, is contained in Appendix A to this manual. Though it is, of course, very ECIS-specific, it contains much that is broadly applicable, particularly in its recommendations for school heads and librarians towards a practical programme to implement improvements in library function. The appendix, thus, should be regarded as an integral part of the manual.

The final stage of the project has been the production of this document. Because it must be pertinent to such a wide variety of institutions, in many different settings, and with different curricular programmes, educational goals, and governance structures, ranging from the barely minimal to the enviably extensive, it is not prescriptive in intent. Instead, it attempts to identify elements and concerns crucial to all good libraries, to make helpful suggestions, to propose a course by which individual schools can arrive at a level of facilities and services appropriate to its own institutional resources and needs.

Nor is the manual a finished exercise, to be read, absorbed and stored away. It is meant to be the basis of a working document which each school will use to develop its own programme, adding the specific bits and pieces pertinent to the particular operation, available for constant reference, updating and modification as schools develop and circumstances change. Thus it has been produced in loose-leaf form, to encourage its continuing use and adaptation, so that, in the course of time, each institution will have, it is hoped, its own 'bible' pertinent to the philosophy and operation of the library of that unique institution.

Finally, it remains to acknowledge again the support given to the project by the Overseas Schools Advisory council, whose members are corporate officers of far-sighted multinational concerns which recognise the vital importance of international schools in the global enterprise in which we are all, in one fashion or another, engaged. Their generous help, organised through the good offices of Dr Ernest Mannino and his colleagues of the Office of Overseas Schools of the US Department of State, and efficiently administered by Dr Samuel Sava and the National Association of Elementary School Principals Foundation, is deeply appreciated by ECIS and all those who have been and will be the grateful beneficiaries of their vision and concern. Specifically, the following Overseas Schools Advisory Council members (*) and US corporations and foundations participated in the grant which made this project possible:

* Bank of America
* Bechtel Power Corporation
  Becton Dickinson Foundation
* Chase Manhattan Bank
* E I Du Pont De Nemours & Co
* Exxon Education Foundation
* Ford Motor Company
* General Electric Foundation
* General Motors
* Goodyear International
  Corporation
* IBM
  McGraw-Hill Foundation Inc
  Merrill Lynch
* Mobil Oil Corporation
  Morrison-Knudsen Engineers Inc

New York Times Company
  Foundation Inc
* Pfizer International Inc
  Phelps Dodge
* Raytheon Company
* RCA Corporation
  Rockwell International
    Corporation Trust
  Schering-Plough Corporation
  Texas Instruments Foundation
  Texas Iron Works, Inc
* US Department of State
* Westinghouse Electric
  Foundation

W G Mattern
Executive Secretary, ECIS
1987